Quality Costing

Quality Costing

Barrie G. Dale
Senior Lecturer and Director
UMIST Quality Management Centre
Manchester

and

James J. Plunkett
Late Total Quality Management Project Officer
UMIST Quality Management Centre
Manchester

CHAPMAN & HALL
London · New York · Tokyo · Melbourne · Madras

UK   Chapman & Hall, 2–6 Boundary Row, London SE1 8HN

USA   Van Nostrand Reinhold, 115 5th Avenue, New York NY10003

JAPAN   Chapman & Hall Japan, Thomson Publishing Japan,
            Hirakawacho Nemoto Building, 7F, 1–7–11 Hirakawa-cho,
            Chiyoda-ku, Tokyo 102

AUSTRALIA   Chapman & Hall Australia, Thomas Nelson Australia,
            102 Dodds Street, South Melbourne, Victoria 3205

INDIA   Chapman & Hall India, R. Seshadri, 32 Second Main Road.
            CIT East, Madras 600 035

First edition 1991

© 1991 Barrie G. Dale and James J. Plunkett

Typeset in 10/12 Palatino by Input Typesetting Ltd
Printed in Great Britain by Page Bros (Norwich) Ltd

ISBN 0 412 38860 X   0 442 31369 1 (USA)

British Library Cataloguing in Publication Data
Dale, Barrie G.
   Quality costing.
   1. Quality control
   I. Title II. Plunkett, J. J.
   658.562

ISBN 0–412–38860–X

Library of Congress Cataloging-in-Publication Data
Dale, B. G.
      Quality costing / Barrie G. Dale and James J. Plunkett.—1st ed.
      p. cm.
      Includes bibliographical references and index.
      ISBN 0–442–31369–1
      1. Quality control—Costs. 2. Quality control—Costs—Case
   studies. 3. Manufactures—Quality control—Case studies.
   I. Plunkett, James J. II. Title.
   TS156.D34 1991   90–49713
   658.5'62—dc20   CIP

Contents

Preface

This book is one of the few English language texts devoted to the subject of quality costing. The material is based on research work carried out by the authors at the Manchester School of Managememt, UMIST, over the last nine years or so. The research has been mainly in manufacturing organizations but work has also been conducted in non-manufacturing concerns (e.g. marketing and service operations, and commerce).

The book will provide managers with sound practical advice on how to define, collect, analyse, report and use quality costs. The text covers all the main aspects of quality costing and an attempt has been made to structure the book in the sequence by which organizations should set about a quality costing exercise.

The book opens by examining the background of quality costing. This is followed by chapters on definitions of quality costs, collection of quality costs, analysis and reporting of quality costs, and the uses of quality costs. Examples from manufacturing organizations and non-manufacturing situations are used throughout the first five chapters to illustrate the key points discussed in the text. The next four chapters are case studies which provide considerable detail on quality costing in companies from the mechanical and electronics industries. To preserve anonymity the companies are not referred to by name. The case studies illustrate how four different companies have set about analysing their main areas of operation to highlight where quality costs were incurred and how they were collected and reported. A deliberate attempt is made to present the situation as encountered by the authors. In this way, potential cost collectors can gain some insight into the type of situations and difficulties they may encounter and the issues which need to be resolved in undertaking a quality costing exercise. The case studies also include guidance on potential sources of cost information and the typical questions which occur in a quality cost collection exercise. The final chapter is a summary of the previous nine and provides guidance on how companies can go about setting up a quality costing system.

There is considerable interest from Western manufacturing industry, public sector organizations, commerce, and the service sector in the subject of total quality management (TQM) and the process of quality improvement. However, the majority of organizations, certainly in the first few years of the TQM journey, do need to justify the cost-effectiveness of the investment in a process of continuous quality improvement to their main board, in particular when it is located in an offshore country, and to shareholders. Consequently, an increasing number of organizations are now actively engaged in the collection and reporting of quality costs and others are looking for sound practical advice on how to go about it. It is also not uncommon to find organizations who, after collecting and using the results of quality costing for some years, wish to critical-analyse their activities in order to make more use of the data.

This book provides useful advice to organizations setting out on a quality costing exercise and to those in the early stages of designing a quality cost collection and reporting system and will help to prevent cost collectors going up blind alleys. It will also assist those organizations already collecting costs by giving pointers on how to develop and refine their current methods.

The book will prove useful to practitioners, academics, and undergraduate and postgraduate students from a variety of disciplines; total quality management is not restricted to one group of people or discipline. People studying for professional examinatons which involve aspects of TQM will also find the book to be of benefit. Quality managers, technical managers, technical specialists and accountants should find the book of particular interest as they are usually the personnel involved in quality costing. The Chief Executive Officer and board members will also benefit from reading the book; they will see in the text hard evidence of the financial benefits accruing to an organization from pursuing a process of continuous quality improvement.

Dr Jim Plunkett, after a brave fight against cancer, died mid-way through the preparation of this book. The book is dedicated to the memory of Jim and provides some recognition of his first-class research into the subject of quality costing.

B. G. Dale
Manchester School of Management, UMIST

1
Quality costing: an introduction

1.1 The role of quality costing in total quality management

In the last decade many Western organizations have come to appreciate the strategic importance of total quality management (TQM) to their corporate health. They have realized that TQM will enable them to become and remain competitive in home and international markets. Consequently, a process of continuous quality improvement has been started.

There are many definitions of TQM. The Japanese do not like, or even use, the term. Instead they refer to company-wide quality control or total quality control; see Ishikawa [1]. Despite the divergence of views on what constitutes TQM there are a number of common threads running through the various definitions. These include: everyone in the organization is involved in improving on a continuous and never-ending basis the processes under their control; each person is committed to satisfying their internal and external customers; teamwork is practised in a number of forms; the development of employees through involvement; participation by everyone in the business is positively encouraged and practised; and customers and suppliers are integrated into the improvement process.

The organizational goal is TQM and the process of quality improvement is the means of reaching this goal. It is important for an organization to understand that in today's markets customer requirements are becoming increasingly more rigorous and at the same time it is likely that their competition will also be improving. Consequently there is a need for the process of quality improvement to be continuous and total. The organization which claims they have achieved TQM will be overtaken by the competition. Once the process of quality improvement has been halted, under the mistaken belief that TQM has been achieved and the ideal state reached, it is much harder to restart the process and gain the initiative on the competition. This is why TQM should always be referred to as a process and not a programme.

Starting a process of quality improvement and then developing and fostering its advancement should be a long-term organizational objective: it often takes at least ten years to put the basics into place. There are no quick fixes, one quality management technique and/or tool which is a panacea for all quality ills and is more important than another, short cuts, and ready-made packages which can be plugged in to guarantee success. Continuous quality improvement requires patience, tenacity, and considerable commitment from people at every level in the organization, in particular the board of directors and senior management team.

It requires some considerable effort to sustain the process of continuous quality improvement and, more often than not, the management of Western organizations will have to justify to their parent company, board and shareholders that the investment in the improvement process is cost-effective. Some people may argue that there should be no need to justify investment in quality improvement activities. We disagree with this view. The environment in the West is such that organizations and their managements are judged over relatively short time periods; indeed this is one of the criticisms often made of executives – that they place too much emphasis on short-term objectives. Committing huge expenditure in quality improvement activities without some measure of its cost-effectiveness can be considered a blind act of faith and is contrary to the way in which Western businesses operate. In Japanese organizations the situation is quite different. Investment in improvement initiatives over a long period of time without thought of immediate benefits appears to be accepted without question by senior managers, shareholders and financial institutions. The Japanese have considerable tangible evidence over the last 30 years or so of pursuing the wisdom of this long-range view.

In addition to product and service quality, organizations need to be competitive on cost and delivery (QCD) and a considerable number of organizations need to achieve substantial cost reductions if they are to survive. Many organization are vulnerable to any breakthrough in rival organizations in relation to quality improvement and technology. In many instances quality-related costs are a major potential source of the necessary savings. Quality costing is one of several tools and techniques which can assist companies with improving product and service quality.

Whilst there is clearly a good case for quality costing, it is not a panacea for quality problems and must not be treated as an end in itself. It is also important that reducing the level of quality costs should not be the main reason for an organization starting a process of quality improvement. Quality costing may be considered by some to be more useful for organizations taking the first steps along the TQM journey than it is for those who have considerably more operating experience of TQM and have had first-hand experience of the benefits of becoming a total quality organization. However, a number of world-class organizations do employ quality costing measures as an indication of internal quality performance.

A knowledge of quality costs helps managers to justify the investment in quality improvement and assists them in monitoring the effectiveness of the efforts made. Quality costing expresses an organization's quality performance in the language of the board, the senior management team, shareholders and financial institutions – money. It is often found that boards and senior management teams are unmoved by quality assurance data but are spurred into action when the same data are expressed and presented in monetary terms. Operators and line supervision are also found to react positively when non-conformance data, in addition to the normally expressed measure of numbers and percentages, are presented in monetary terms. This happens when they have the opportunity to compare the costs of non-conformance with their salaries.

Sullivan [2, 3], in an issue of *Quality Progress* (the Journal of the American Society of Quality Control) devoted to quality costs, quotes half a dozen 'top quality professionals' in support of quality costing and also Claret [4] and Cox [5], from the accounting fraternity, acknowledge the need for quality costing. The following are some comments made by Chief Executive Officers in The Department of Trade and Industry booklet *The Case For Costing Quality* by Dale and Plunkett [6].

> Quality costs allow us to identify the soft targets to which we can apply our improvement efforts.
>
> John Asher, Managing Director, Crown Industrial Products

> Four years ago we could still use quality as a selling feature for our product, now that's all changed. If you are still a supplier to the automotive industry today, you will have achieved a high level of quality that is the accepted norm in the industry. Those companies who have failed to improve their quality are no longer suppliers. Customers expect to share in the benefits of our continuous quality improvement efforts through agreed cost reduction programmes and extended warranty agreements. Without tracking quality costs we could seriously impair our bottom line profitability and not know the reason why.
>
> Tony Harman, Managing Director, Garrett Automotive (*Turbocharger division*)

With the prospect of increased competition as a result of activities surrounding 1992, it is important for us to continually improve our operational methods. The formal measurement of quality costs is central to that process, and has the added benefit of showing us how we can tackle certain areas of costs.

John Barbour, Managing Director, John Russell (Grangemouth) Ltd

Quality must be one of the cornerstones for a growing company, otherwise spectacular growth can be followed by an equally rapid descent and quality costs are one of the measures by which this can be monitored.

Ian Elliot, Managing Director, Pirelli Focom

From the foregoing discussion one might imagine that no company could afford to be without a quality cost collection system. Not so: many organizations have no form of quality costing and many managers do not understand the concept. In 1971 the Department of Trade and Industry (Mensforth [7]) recorded disappointment at how few firms collect and analyse quality costs. More recent surveys by Roche [8] and Duncalf and Dale [9] showed that only about one-third of the companies they studied collect quality costs. From the research work carried out by the authors on the subject of quality costing over the last nine years or so they confirm these findings; it is believed that less than 40% of companies collect and measure their quality costs in a systematic manner. In most cases only the costs of scrap, rework and warranty claims are measured. For example, a major supplier of clothing to a retailing company with a first-class reputation for the quality of its goods does not measure quality costs. Discussions revealed that its senior management appear to think that the company's ability to satisfy such a quality-conscious customer at competitive prices shows that they are running a tight ship. This is in spite of having a large 'seconds' shop at the factory site and considering opening three High Street outlets for sales of 'seconds'. On a more positive note, all the signs are that the interest from organizations in the concept of quality costing is growing. A number of organizations are now seeking and getting practical evidence on quality-related costs and others are developing formalized quality costing systems.

Inevitably there are those who question or oppose the consensus view in relation to quality costing. Sitting [10] maintains there are no such things as quality costs, but he concedes that it is important to analyse the relationship between total production cost (including quality costs) and quality. Tsiakals [11] warns that quality cost reporting alone does not impove quality and reduce costs. Neither does quality cost analysis. Morse [12], writing from an accountant's viewpoint, also warns that organizations should not expect too much from the quality costing activity. Some people hold the view that the measurement of quality costs can actually deflect attention from their reduction and be detrimental to quality improvement. We have no evidence to support or refute this point of view. There is no ideal way of starting, developing and fostering quality improvement; each organization is different in terms of processes, products, history, culture and people and what works well in one situation may not necessarily be as effective in another. The same can be said to be true of quality costing and organizations must make up their own minds on the value of the quality costing concept to the process of continuous quality improvement.

1.2 What are quality costs?

There is by no means a uniform view of what is meant by a quality cost and what should be included under the quality cost umbrella. Definitions are a key feature in quality costing and Chapter 2 is devoted to this topic. Ideas of what constitutes quality costs have been changing rapidly in recent years. Whereas only a few years ago the costs of quality were perceived as the cost of running the quality assurance department, plus scrap and warranty costs, it is now widely accepted that they are the costs incurred in the design, implementation, operation and maintenance of an organization's quality system, the cost of organizational resources committed to the process of continuous quality improvement, and the costs of system, product and service failures.

Quality systems may range from simple inspection to systems surpassing the requirements of the BS 5750/ISO 9000 series [13] or any other recognized quality system standard, (i.e. The Ford Motor Company World wide, Quality System Standard Q–101 [14]). System failures can result in obsolescent stocks, lost items, production or operation delays, additional work, scrap, rectification work, late deliveries, additional transportation costs, poor service, and non-conforming products. Product and/or service failures result in warranty, guarantee and product liability claims, complaint administration and investigation, product recall, additional customer service costs, and loss of customer goodwill.

So quality-related costs are not, as is sometimes thought, just the cost of quality assurance, inspection, monitoring, test and scrap materials, components and products. Quality-related costs arise from a range of activities and involve a number of departments in an organization, all of which impinge on the quality of the product or service. For example:

- sales and marketing;
- design, research and development
- purchasing, storage, handling;
- production or operations planning and control;

- manufacturing/operations;
- delivery, installation;
- service.

Nor are they wholly determined or controlled from within an organization. Suppliers, subcontractors, stockists, agents, dealers and customers can all influence the incidence and level of quality-related costs.

1.3 Quality costs and in-built inefficiencies

When considering the nitty-gritty of quality costs there is considerable controversy about which activities and costs are quality related. Many quality-related costs are excess production/operation costs arising from the inability to 'get things right first time'. Considerable potential savings can be identified by examining closely the costs of quality-related operations themselves, e.g. inspection, auditing, guarantee and warranty undertakings.

Many in-built inefficiencies such as excess materials allowances, excess paper and forms, excess production/operations starts, and deliberate overmakes, though not regarded specifically as production and operating costs, may in fact have their origins in engineering, technical, manufacturing and operating inefficiency. The same may also be true of the provision of standby machines, equipment and personnel, additional supervision, and some safety stocks and items. Similarly, in an engineering situation, excess and selective fitting owing to variability of machined parts is often an accepted practice. This can be considerably reduced or even eliminated by the use of statistical process control (SPC).

Snagging facilities to avoid stopping production in line manufacturing are another form of in-built inefficiency. An example met with in the authors' research work was in the manufacture of engines. Sometimes it is not possible to complete assemblies because the requisite components are not available at the assembly line. Hence incomplete engines are diverted to a snagging area where finishing is carried out, e.g. fitting fuel pumps or starter motors. The quality assurance manager at the site maintained that the cost of the facility was a quality cost, and specifically a failure cost. His reasoning was that the snagging operation is necessary because there has been a failure somewhere in the system and that the cost of compensating for the failure is a quality cost. Many people would reason that because systems are imperfect it is necessary to provide contingency facilities, such as snagging areas, and that their operating costs are just another built-in burden. However, there is no reason why the principle of accountability should not apply and the function responsible for the failure (purchasing, stores, planning, materials management, etc.) made accountable for the cost.

Lack of attention to maintenance of process and equipment performance may result in built-in costs by the acceptance of inadequate levels of capability and more non-conformances than are necessary. Maintenance budgets are frequently decided on an arbitrary or general experience basis without taking due regard of the particular process needs. Maintenance should be preventive in the sense of prevention of non-conformances rather than preventing breakdown. Failure to do this is tantamount to building in unnecessarily high levels of non-conformance with consequential in-built costs. Japanese companies have been actively pursing total productive maintenance (TPM) for a number of years. This philosophy recognizes that machines and equipment are a key determinant of production and operation quality and it is people who maintain machines and improve their efficiency and effectiveness. Consequently, TPM encourages the involvement of everyone in this activity. For further details of TPM see Nakajima [15].

In engineering-type situations, excess use of materials for starts, ends, and offcuts are built-in manufacturing costs which arise from inattention to details of the process. Wastage of materials on starts can be reduced by using scrap or cheaper materials, and end wastage can be minimized by accurately counting the output and stopping (as opposed to running down) the producing machinery. Non-conformances may be minimized by careful attention to the available standard dimensions of raw materials and to techniques such as computer-aided nesting to utilize fully the available material.

The principal problem arising from built-in inefficiencies, apart from their direct costs, is that they distort the base values against which important judgements are made and, ironically, the more the base values are used the more firmly entrenched and accepted the built-in efficiencies become.

1.4 Quality costs and delivery performance

A cause of poor quality which is not usually specified, but which is widely acknowledged, arises from the quality–delivery dilemma. Sometimes quality is only achieved at the expense of a default on delivery, or vice versa. Manufacturers of large heavy goods for overseas customers especially can face very severe quality cost penalties if agreed shipping dates are not met; the same is true in the construction industry. Having to compromise also tends to increase the amount of products passed-on concession, and tends to increase inventory levels.

In the contexts of accounting, contract work, and other matters with terminal dates or deadlines, there is often an implicit acceptance of a lower standard of quality provided the deadline is met. Thus, for example, accountants furnish estimates if exact data are not available, and there are greater numbers of errors in latest news articles than in feature articles in newspapers, etc. Perhaps it is similar evidence of the effects on quality on tipping the balance in favour of delivery, which makes organizations try hard to maintain a more balanced situation.

The quality–delivery dilemma is probably an important factor in the poor delivery performance of some organizations, even though, according to the quality fraternity, goods often progress through to delivery with indecent haste. On the other hand, production and operations people complain constantly that quality considerations impede output and the meeting of production schedules.

There is probably some truth in the assertion that production and operations people use quality as an excuse for poor delivery. This might be credible if deliveries were a matter of hours, or even days, late. But when deliveries are weeks, or even months, behind schedule for supposedly quality-related reasons, the implications are that the company must have serious quality problems and one wonders what the cost consequences might have been if the quality procedures had been bypassed to deliver on time.

1.5 A short history of quality costing

It was the Americans who first identified and defined quality costs. However, definitions of quality-related costs have changed as perceptions of TQM and quality improvement have changed and it is difficult to determine when quality-related costs were first referred to as such. Almost all the early papers on quality mention only inspection, rework, repair, and warranty costs (i.e. elements of what are now called appraisal and failure categories of quality-related costs). The term 'quality costs' was certainly in use in Western Europe in the early 1960s and may have originated with the categorization of costs into prevention–appraisal–failure, which is attributed to the seminal paper of Feigenbaum [16] in the mid 1950s.

In 1967 the American Society for Quality Control (ASQC) published *Quality Costs – What and How* [17] in which quality costs are defined only by category and by reference to Feigenbaum. This booklet, which was revised in 1970 and 1974, is still perhaps the most definitive work on the subject, even though it does not include all the cost elements which might be identified as being quality related in a total approach to the management of product and service quality. It takes the 'What' concept and quality cost definitions from Feigenbaum's book *Total Quality Control* [18], but adds sources for finding cost data and gives a lot of good advice on what to include, what to leave out, and specific warnings to be cautious in interpreting and using cost data. However, only about one-third of the book is taken up with quality cost definitions. The rest is about getting management attention and approval, cost collection and tabulation, quality cost trend analysis and corrective analysis, business reports to management, and audit and follow-up. In short, the emphasis is on the use of cost information.

The style of presentation is such that the booklet is helpful and encouraging rather than authoritative and dictatorial in getting its message across. The booklet's messages are spelled out simply and clearly (though perhaps too wordily for some) and are supplemented with plenty of illustrative charts and exhibits with explanatory notes. The reader is led gently but firmly along the path of getting approximate costs to attract management attention and approval of a quality cost programme, involving other departments, selection of an initial project, definition of cost elements, collection, analysis, presentation, reporting to management, audit and follow-up, with lots of good advice along the way. The fact that the emphasis is on measuring and reducing (or optimizing) the major quality cost categories and elements, rather than on the currently more popular quality cost improvement projects approach, does not invalidate or detract from the value of the strategy or advice in any way.

Other ASQC publications which deal best with practical aspects on how to do quality costing are *Guide for Reducing Quality Costs* [19] and *Guide for Managing Supplier Quality Costs* [20].

The *Guide for Reducing Quality Costs* (the first edition was published seven years later than *Quality Costs – What and How*) develops the uses of quality costing by directing attention to quality improvement projects and to the involvement and responsibilities of technical, marketing and purchasing functions in quality matters. It deals with identifying problem areas and analysis of quality costs. It makes specific recommendations on reducing failure and appraisal costs, prevention of quality costs, and measuring improvement, as well as providing case study examples. The idea of projecting failure and appraisal costs as desirable targets for cost reduction but regarding prevention as a cost-saving activity is a commendable one. Under the heading 'prevention of quality costs' are listed ways in which marketing, design, quality assurance, and indeed management, in general, can help to prevent appraisal and failure costs from arising.

The *Guide for Managing Supplier Quality Costs* (the first edition was published three years later than the *Guide for Reducing Quality Costs*) is an acknowledgement of the fact that companies purchase some of their quality problems. Today, many major Western organizations are now devoting considerable resources in developing their relationships with supplier communities and working more closely with them on quality improvement initiatives. The guide wastes no time before getting down to methods of vendor control, the visible and hidden quality costs related to vendor control, and methods of applications of quality cost to vendor control. The instruction and advice is detailed, specific and clear, as in the other two ASQC publications. Two themes are pursued, identifying and attacking vendor-related problems through joint projects with the vendor and motivating the vendor to adopt his own quality cost programme.

All three of the booklets are excellent publications and should be compulsory reading for anyone undertaking work on the collection and use of quality-related costs. The only major criticism to be made of these three publicatons is that the whole emphasis is on reducing costs. Nowhere is mooted the alternative approach of improving product and service quality without increasing costs. Many companies regard product and service quality as being of such prime importance that they are unwilling to put it at risk for the purpose of cost reductions. Indeed, some companies are looking to quality expenditures as areas for profitable investment.

The British Standards Institution's publication – BS 6143 *Guide to the Determination and Use of Quality Related Costs* [21] (1981 issue) – is in many respects an abridged version of *Quality Costs – What and How*; it is but a poor imitation. The stated primary intention is to provide guidance on the operation of a quality costs system within a manufacturing organization. As judged by the list of contents, the guide promises much, but it fails to deliver on these promises. The presentation of the Standard does not engender a flexible approach to collecting costs, even though it may have been intended. BS 6143 does not reflect accurately the incidence and distribution of costs in manufacturing industry and non-manufacturing situations as encountered in the authors' researches. The emphasis in the Standard reflects the magnitude of quality activities rather than quality-related costs. The flaws in the Standard are discussed in some detail by Plunkett and Dale [22].

Whilst there is little doubt that many of the faults of the Standard derive from the abridging process, it also bears one of the hallmarks of committee work. How else would prevention activities which account for say 2% of quality costs (BS 6143 'typical data') be broken down into eight minutely detailed elements whilst internal failure costs (63% of quality costs – same data source) though having seven elements are not analysed in nearly so much detail? In another instance, an example cites 14 prevention elements, six appraisal, seven internal failure and five external failure elements. All in all, users would have been better served if the committee had adopted the ASQC's *Quality Costs – What and How* and incorporated material from the other two publications, though it has to be admitted that the style and content of such a document would be unusual for a British Standard.

Many of these criticisms have been taken into account in an extensive revision of the standard by the Quality Management and Statistics Standard Policy Committee. The standard which is now titled *Guide to the Economics of Quality* [23] is published in two parts. To cater for non-manufacturing situations and for those organizations wishing to pursue an alternative approach to the prevention–appraisal–failure (PAF) model the first part of the guide comprises a process cost modelling approach. The second part is a revised version of the classical PAF model.

Quality costing has been primarily used by manufacturing industry, but today there is growing interest from commerce, the public sector and service-related organizations. Dale and Plunkett [6] describe the use made of quality costing by British Airways Technical Workshops (the workshops are responsible for the overhaul and repair of items removed from aircraft), John Russell (Grangemouth) (a transportation and warehousing company) and National Westminster Bank. It is interesting to note that National Westminster Bank refer to quality costing as the cost of making mistakes.

1.6 Why are quality costs important?

Firstly, because they are large, very large. In 1978 they were estimated by the UK Government to be £10 000 million, equal to 10% of the UK's gross national product (GNP). There is no reason to suppose that they are any less now. The findings of a NEDO task force on quality and standards, published in 1985 [24], claims that some 10 to 20% of an organization's total sales value is accounted for by quality-related costs and, using the figure of 10%, it is estimated that UK manufacturing industry could save up to £6 billion each year by reducing such costs. Various studies and information volunteered to the authors by a variety of organizations have shown that quality-related costs commonly range from 5 to 25% of company annual sales turnover. The costs depend on the type of industry, business situation or service, the view taken by the organization of what is or is not a quality-related cost, the approach to TQM, and the extent to which continuous quality improvement is practised in the organization.

Secondly, 95% of the quality cost is usually expended on appraisal and failure. These expenditures add little to the value of the product or service, and the failure costs, at least, may be regarded as avoidable. Reducing failure cost by eliminating causes of non-conformance can also lead to substantial reductions in appraisal costs. The authors' research evidence suggests that quality-related costs may be reduced to one-third of their present level, within a period of three years, by the commitment of the organization to a process of continuous quality improvement.

Thirdly, unnecessary and avoidable costs make goods and services more expensive. This in turn affects competitiveness and, ultimately, wages, salaries and standards of living.

Fourthly, despite the fact that the costs are large, and that a substantial proportion of them are avoidable, it is apparent that the costs and economics of many quality-related activities, including investment in prevention and appraisal activities, are not known by companies. Such a state of affairs is surely indefensible in any well-run business.

1.7 Published quality cost data

In this context data mean real numbers. The literature is strewn with numbers, many of them fictitious. It is not always easy to tell the difference. Some examples may use real figures under fictitious company names. It should be noted that much of what has been written on quality costs is of a qualitative nature and that, with few exceptions, the quantitative data are broad and unqualified. However, so far as the authors are able to judge, what now follows in the text relates to real numbers.

The literature which contains numerical quality cost data falls conveniently into three groups: (1) figures of costs for quality to nations and multi-national corporations, (2) comparisons between industries and industry groups, and (3) individual company experience.

1.7.1 Costs of quality relating to nations and multi-national corporations

From the first group, MacGregor [25] puts the ubiquitous UK quality cost of £10 000 million per year (1978 prices) into perspective when he equates it to the income from value-added tax (VAT) plus the income from tourism and North Sea oil. He also quotes an unnamed major international industrial company achieving annual savings of $22 million rising to $42 million over five years by eliminating quality problems. Wheelwright and Hayes [26] reveal that IBM's quality costs in the early 1980s were 30% of their manufacturing costs. Rohan [27] from the aircraft industry, where costs are huge anyway, discloses that despite an annual expenditure of $30 million on quality assurance, defects and other quality problems were costing the Fairchild Republic Co. a further $20 million each year. After getting to grips with the problems they reduced quality-related losses by more than 80%. Mayben [28] from military aircraft manufacture is less forthcoming about expenditure and losses but returns on investment of quality improvements ranging from 2:1 to 20:1, and on one project an estimated saving of $11 million over ten years, make impressive reading. For sheer awesomeness of quality costs and savings ITT are well to the front and even Jones' [29] $30 million of quality cost improvements planned for 1977 seems small when compared with Groocock's [30] reported $460 million and $550 million quality costs in 1978 and 1979 respectively for the European operation alone.

1.7.2 Costs of quality comparisons between industries and industry groups

Information showing quality cost levels and distributions of expenditure are useful if only to reinforce the warnings about comparisons of data. The periodical *Quality* [31] reporting data across 11 industry groups, at two levels of sophistication of cost collection and expressed against two bases (net sales billed and direct labour), shows clearly the folly of attempting to make comparisons across industry boundaries. The only cross-industry research known to the authors' is by Gilmore [32–34] in which he investigates ten industry groups, different company sizes, and production to quality personnel ratios, looking for differences in total quality costs and in prevention–appraisal–failure distributions.

Robertson [35] draws on data of the National Council for Quality and Reliability saying that for the average UK organization quality-related costs are divided 65% failure costs, 30% appraisal costs, 5% prevention costs; that they may be 4–20% of sales turnover; and that concentrating on prevention may alter the failure–appraisal–prevention ratio to 35:20:10 whilst achieving savings of 1.5 to 6.5% of sales turnover.

Abed and Dale (36) from an analysis of the quantitative data contained in the quality costing literature found that the quality cost categories expressed as a percentage of total quality costs are failure 67%, appraisal 28% and prevention 5%, and total quality costs as a percentage of sales turnover averaged 9.2% with a range from 2 to 25%.

1.7.3 Costs of quality from individual companies

Contributions from individual companies are valuable because many reveal how they measured quality costs and how they achieved their cost reductions. Revealing actual data gives their contributions an authenticity lacking in papers without data. Richardson's [37] paper from the engineering industry is an excellent example. Starting with one in six of the total complement of personnel on the quality budget and a reject rate of 6% giving quality costs of 13.2% of sales turnover, the company reduced the personnel in its quality assurance function from 125 to 35 whilst defect rates fell from 6% to 4% through a series of quality improvement activities giving around 10% of annual sales turnover – worth £1 million – as real savings. Add in enhancement of the company's price competitiveness owing to the savings, and its improved ability to respond to order requirements because of the obvious reduction in lead time, and one is left with a story which spells success by any standards. Paradoxically, this success was achieved by applying the quality assurance manager's joke 'We can reduce our quality costs tomorrow – just sack the inspectors and checkers'.

Garvin [38] using the example of air-conditioning equipment notes that Japanese manufacturers warranty costs are about 0.6% of sales turnover. At the best American companies it was 1.8%; at the worst 5.2%. Further, the total costs of quality incurred by Japanese producers were less than one-half of the failure costs incurred by the best American companies.

From a survey and study in the machine-tool industry, Burns [39] reports quality costs as 5% of estimated sales turnover, of which approximately 60% were failure costs. The proportions of measured quality costs falling into the main categories of quality costs were prevention 3.3%, appraisal 40.3%, failure 56.3%. This level of prevention investment was compared with a level of 13% claimed from a similar survey carried out in West Germany. From the company in which Burns carried out a detailed case study he reports a reduction in quality costs of 1.6% of sales turnover between the year of measurement (1970) and a post-study audit of 1973 costs.

Webb [40] compares meat processing industry costs with general industry costs as shown in Table 1.1.

Table 1.1 Comparison of meat processing industry with general industry costs

	General industry (%)	Meat industry (%)
Failure	65	79
Appraisal	25	8
Prevention (machinery maintenance, etc.)	8	10
Prevention (technologies, etc.)	2	3
Per cent sales	10	6

British Aerospace Dynamics quality costs are 11% of the total cost of production.

In British Airways Technical Workshops, staff time on quality-related matters are: Failure (22.9%), Prevention (19.4%) and Appraisal (6.8%).

The costs of quality in Courtaulds Jersey have been reduced from 12.1% to 7.6% of sales turnover over a period of 4 years.

The cost of quality in Standfast Dyers and Printers (another Courtaulds company) have been reduced from 20% to 7% of sales turnover over a period of 4 years.

In 1986, the quality costs at Crown Industrial Products were 13% of raw material usage costs, by late 1988 they were down to 8%.

In 1986 the quality costs of Garrett Automotive (Turbocharger Division) were 6.5% of sales turnover, by 1988 they had fallen to 4% of sales turnover.

At Grace Dearborn the cost of quality is 20% of sales turnover.

In 1987 the costs of quality at ICL (Manufacturing and Logistics) were £60M.

In 1988 the costs of quality at John McGavigan were 22% of sales turnover.

At National Westminster Bank, 25% of operating costs is absorbed in the difference between the cost actually incurred in accomplishing a task and the cost of a 'right first time' approach.

Philips Components Blackburn have reduced their plant-wide quality costs by 60% over a period of six years.

The following three contributions by Huckett [42], Krzikowski [43] and Kohl [44] are special because they give quality costs and changing distributions between categories of cost over periods of six to eight years.

Huckett [42] recounts the achievements of the 1984 British Quality Award winners, Rank Xerox, at their Mitcheldean site. Reduction in the cost of quality is one of their key measurements of results and their data show a steady reduction from 6% of manufacturing cost in 1979 to a little over 1% in 1984.

Krzikowski [43] presents an excellently detailed paper on quality in the cash register manufacturing business. He indicates total quality costs as a percentage, probably of manufacturing cost, though it is not specifically stated. However, he shows the changes in distribution of prevention–appraisal–failure costs as the total costs fall from 6.4% to 4.4% over a period of six years. The data are unusual in that prevention costs were increased to a point where they caused the total costs to rise but it is clear from the text that this is entirely due to a one-off training exercise for inspectors.

Kohl [44] from the Allis-Chalmers Corporation claims a 35% reduction in 1970 of 1969 quality costs of $1.6 million, in addition to conserving interest costs by 6.3% by improving cash flow. Over 18 months 'the portion of the specification cost dollar spent on internal failures was also reduced by 2 cents to 7/10 cent' giving a saving of $405 000. At one factory the inspection force was reduced by 43% whilst at another the total costs of quality were reduced by 70%, equivalent to 3% of sales turnover (i.e. from 4.5 to 1.5% of sales turnover). However, by far the most interesting data are the 'allocation of the quality dollar' to prevention–appraisal–failure and the total quality costs for the years

1967 to 1974. These indicate the substantial reduction in total failure costs noted above and an even more dramatic change in the relative expenditures (e.g. external failure costs falling from 46 to 6% of the total whilst prevention expenditure was increased twofold).

1.8 Why measure quality costs?

The measurement of costs allows quality-related activities to be expressed in the language of management. This, in turn, allows quality to be treated as a business parameter along with, for example, marketing, research and development, and production/operations. Drawing quality costs into the business arena helps to emphasize the importance of product and service quality to corporate health and will help to influence employee behaviour and attitudes at all levels in the organization towards TQM and continuous quality improvement.

Quality cost measurement focuses attention on areas of high expenditure and identifies potential cost-reduction opportunities. It allows measurement of performance and provides a basis for internal comparison between products, services, processes and departments. Measurement of quality-related costs also reveals quirks and anomalies in cost allocation and standards which may remain undetected by the more commonly used production/operation and labour-based analyses; it can also highlight fraud. Measurement can also obviate the dumping of embarrassing after-sales costs under quality-related headings.

Finally, and perhaps most importantly, measurement is the first step towards control and improvement.

1.9 Accounting, accountants and quality costing

The initiative to collect and analyse quality costs comes, in general, from the quality assurance department; sometimes it is driven by the board of directors and senior management team but rarely does the initiative come from the accounting and financial department. Initiatives emanating from accountants seem to be prompted only by high costs of inspection and checking or scrap appearing in labour or material cost analyses respectively. The collection of quality costs should be a joint exercise of quality assurance, technical specialists and accountants. Accountants should be involved from the outset of the exercise. The costs should be produced or endorsed by the accounts department who should also be specifically charged with responsibility for avoiding double-counting. Quality assurance and technical specialists frequently complain about the lack of initiative taken and shown by accountants in the quality costing exercise. There is a view that accountants tend to raise barricades in anticipation of an onslaught from quality assurance managers in search of accurate quality costs.

The collection of quality costs, their analysis and reporting is dealt with in Chapters 3 and 4 respectively. However, in this opening chapter it is important to review the contribution, or lack of it, by accountants to the subject of quality costing.

The accountancy literature contains few articles on quality costs. A few contributions worth noting have been found and are reported here together with some views of accountants and accountancy from the quality assurance and management literature.

Jorgensen [45] was clearly unhappy with his local accountancy department, and its staff when he wrote that

> the accounting systems in most factories are built upon rather conservative principles, which rarely provide for the instant and relevant information necessary to run a quality control department.
>
> A great amount of energy and tact is necessary on the part of the Quality Control Department in order to overcome this difficulty . . . quality control must make a habit of using the data from traditional accountancy with a great amount of suspicion and must try to convince the accountants of the justice of this suspicion.

Krzikowski [43] was equally gloomy when he noted that

> an exact calculation of the quality costs would demand a radical change in the Accounts Department – as radical as the introduction of the accounting systems in German companies about 30 year ago.

Jorgensen and Krzikowski were writing 20 years ago. But ten years later Brown [46] still felt constrained in his ability to give guidance on establishing and controlling quality costs, thus:

> Unfortunately, due to the differences in accounting procedures within industry, it is not possible to lay down hard and fast rules for establishing and controlling quality costs. This paper sets down the basic principles behind any quality cost investigation, bearing in mind that the procedures and make-up of costs will vary as the accounting procedures vary.

But it suggests that the gap between engineer and accountant was getting narrower.

At about the same time Mandel [47] was offering a statistician's alternative to cost accountancy – random time sampling. Referring to the inability of conventional cost accounting systems to provide the special type of cost information required for quality costing, especially with respect to personnel and machine costs, he suggests 'an effective and efficient method of costing, called random time sampling, exists which meets the costing requirements of relevance, accuracy, simplicity, and economy' and it has been found to be 'a highly acceptable alternative to the conventional cost accounting system'. It is also less subjective, and cheaper, but it does not appear to have caught on so far as can be gauged from published information on quality costing systems.

Olson [48] found that the company's accounting department benefited from his improvement to a discrepant materials reporting and action system by generating information it could not get previously. He cites an example that on one single day there was a total of $160 000 worth of rejected materials and parts. Apparently that information could not have been available before, and must be of considerable value to company management. A very important point emerging from this is that cost data cannot be any better than the underlying time or materials or labour data. If these are uncontrolled there is no way they can be costed properly.

Hallum and Casperson [49] appear to have a good working relationship with accountants in their organization. They open their paper with a description of their accounting system. Costs carry three labels, the kind of costs (e.g. wages, salaries, materials), the place of the cost or the department debited, and the purpose of the cost (e.g. production, sales, product development, quality-control, etc.) which makes life much easier for them when collecting quality costs, though no doubt there are some misallocations through wrong labelling and differences of opinion about the purposes of expenditures. Ironically they work for the same company whose accountants were so distrusted by Jorgensen 12 years before.

In the special quality costs edition of *Quality Progress*, Sullivan [2] reports a member of the ASQC's Quality Costs Technical Committee as saying

> The emphasis in quality costs is to get the accounting people involved

and that the committee

> has been in contact with representatives of professional associations of accountants to develop better ways of capturing quality costs.
>
> If the system is properly explained, finance and accounting departments are generally glad to help set up a cost system, according to Feigenbaum 'This gives them the opportunity to measure major costs that just haven't been measured'.

There is little doubt that during the last 20 years or so there has been a considerable change in attitude towards accountants and what may be expected of them.

In the opposite corner, whilst not writing a great deal about quality costs, the accountants have some worthy champions of their cause. Morse [12] shows a sensitivity to the problems of gaining the cooperation of quality assurance personnel when he writes of the inappropriateness of the expression 'cost of quality' (as opposed to quality costs) in that it implies a trade-off between cost and quality, and of the effects its use is likely to have. None the less he is firm in the accountants' assertion that the ultimate purpose of a quality cost system is to give management a means of planning and controlling costs.

Cox [50] looks at quality from the point of view of the community at large, from the user's standpoint and from that of the manufacturer and/or provider. For the user he identifies aspects of product failure which cannot be quantified in money terms but result in a loss to the manufacturer in terms of negative goodwill. For the manufacturer and provider he points out that whilst anything spent on achieving conformance to specification represents a charge against profits (and hence the manufacturer's/provider's objective must be to minimize quality costs for the particular (specification) sometimes he has no choice as to how much he must spend. For example, products which are likely to cause severe loss of life or ecological disaster require that the original specification must be right and the quality effort must be absolute. The possibility of death or injury to individuals imposes moral and legal constraints which will require close attention to quality assurance, with relatively high quality-related costs. Only in cases where the only consequence of failure is loss of profit is the manufacturer in a position to trade quality costs against profit. An examination of where a manufacturer's products stand in this quality cost spectrum is an advisable precursor to an organization undertaking a quality costing exercise.

In a second contribution Cox [51] does his profession an excellent service by setting down what a management accountant does. He briefly discusses long-term planning, budgeting and quality costing, and closes on a practical note that the management accounting function has just as many constraints on its resources as any other function and will need to be persuaded that the results obtained from a cost collection exercise are likely to be worth the time and effort. Sensibly too, he warns against expecting accountants to be arbiters in disputes between departments over allocations of costs.

Claret [4], whilst recognising that

> accountants are frequently seen as responsible for many of the ills of society,

is at pains to point out that the accountant does not make the decisions which result in the ills.

He discusses the limitations of the accountant's contribution to quality-related matters and makes some suggestions for improvement. In particular he points out that accountants usually get involved in capital investment but, in many businesses, do not get involved in revenue investment decision (e.g. in production engineering and new designs).

He appeals to accountants to get themselves involved in all kinds of investment decisions and suggests some self-help by urging them to develop models

> which allow them to test the relationships between costs, quality, investment, and improved turnover through improved quality.

The quality assurance profession must look forward with interest to the publication of such a model.

Lastly, Sandretto [52], in a paper which goes much further than Cox's explanation of what management accounting is about, stresses that, although conceptually simple, cost accounting is not an all-purpose management tool. It is very much a matter of horses for courses. Uses of costs information, inputs, outputs and operation constraints, various manufacturing situations (e.g. job order production, discrete part products, few material inputs) and service companies, together with influences of various factors on cost control and analysis and the conflicting needs for control and analysis, are all discussed in a paper which although not specifically on quality costs is excellent exercise.

References

1. Ishikawa, K. (1985) *What is Total Quality Control? The Japanese Way*, Prentice-Hall, Englewood Cliffs, NJ.
2. Sullivan, E. (1983) Quality costs: current ideas. *Qual. Prog.*, **16** (4), 24–25.
3. Sullivan, E. (1983) Quality costs: current applications. *Qual. Prog.*, **16** (4), 34–7.
4. Claret, J. (1981) Never mind the quality. *Manage. Acc.*, May, 24–6.
5. Cox, B. (1982). The role of the management accountant in quality costing. *Qual. Assur.*, **8**, (3), 82–4.
6. Dale, B. G. and Plunkett, J. J. (1990) *The Case for Quality Costing*, Department of Trade and Industry, London.
7. Mensforth, E. (1971) *Report of a Committee on the Means of Authenticating the Quality of Engineering Products and Material*, Department of Trade and Industry, London.
8. Roche, J. G. (1981) *National Survey of Quality Control in Manufacturing Industries*, National Board of Science and Technology, Dublin.
9. Duncalf, A. J. and Dale, B. G. (1985) How British industry is making decisions on product quality. *Long Range Plann.*, **18**, (5), 81–8.
10. Sitting, J. (1963) Defining quality costs, *Proc. 7th EOQC Conf.*, *Copenhagen*, pp. 9–17.
11. Tsiakals, J. J. (1983) Management team seeks quality improvement from quality costs. *Qual. Prog.*, **16** (4), 26–7.

12. Morse, W. J. (1983) Measuring quality costs. *Cost Manage.*, July/August, 16–20.

13. BS 5750/ISO 9000 (1987) *Qual. Syst.*, British Standards Institution, London.

14. Anon (1990) *World wide Quality System Standard*, Q–101 Ford Motor Company, Plymouth, Michigan.

15. Nakajima, S. (1988) *Introduction to Total Productive Maintenance*, Productivity Press, Cambridge, MA.

16. Feigenbaum A. V. (1956) Total quality control. *Harvard Bus. Rev.*, **34**, (6), 93–101.

17. ASQC Quality Costs Committee (1974) *Quality Costs – What and How*, American Society for Quality Control, Milwaukee, WI.

18. Feigenbaum, A. V. (1961) *Total Quality Control*, McGraw-Hill, New York.

19. ASQC Quality Costs Committee (1977) *Guide for Reducing Quality Costs*, American Society for Quality Control, Milwaukee, WI.

20. ASQC Quality Costs Committee (1987) *Guide for Managing Supplier Quality Costs*, American Society for Quality Control, Milwaukee, WI.

21. BS 6143 (1981) *Guide to the Determination and Use of Quality Related Costs*, British Standards Institution, London.

22. Plunkett, J. J. and Dale, B. G. (1988) Quality-related costing: findings from an industry-based research study. *Eng. Manage. Int.*, **4**, (4), 247–57.

23. BS 6143: Parts 1 (1991) and 2 (1990) *Guide to the Economics of Quality*, British Standards Institution, London.

24. Anon (1985) *Quality and Value for Money*, National Economic Development Council, London.

25. MacGregor, A. (1983) Making profit from quality. *Qual. Today*, June, 2–3.

26. Wheelwright, S. C. and Hayes, R. H. (1985) Competing through manufacturing. *Harvard Bus. Rev.*, January/February, 99–109.

27. Rohan, T. M. (1987) Quality or junk? Facing up to the problem. *Ind. Week*, December 12, 72–4 and 78–9.

28. Mayben, J. E. (1983) Quality percepts – new profits from the modern Q.A. program. *Qual. Prog.*, **16**, (1), 24–9.

29. Jones, J. S. (1978) Quality costs and quality improvement. *Chart. Mech. Eng.*, February, 76–7.

30. Groocock, J. M. (1980) Quality-cost control in ITT Europe. *Qual. Assur.*, **6**, (3), 37–44.

31. Anon (1977) Quality cost survey. *Quality*, June, 20–2.

32. Gilmore, H. L. (1974) Product conformance cost. *Qual. Prog.*, June, 16–19.

33. Gilmore, H. L. (1983) Consumer product quality control cost revisited. *Qual. Prog.*, **16**, (4), 28–32.
34. Gilmore, H. L. (1984) Consumer product quality costs, *Proc. the World Quality Congr., Brighton*, pp. 587–95.
35. Robertson, A. G. (1971) *Quality Control and Reliability*, Pitman, London.
36. Abed, M. H. and Dale, B. G. (1987) An attempt to identify quality-related costs in textile manufacturing. *Qual. Assur.*, **13**, (2), 41–5.
37. Richardson, D. W. (1983) Cost benefits of quality control, a practical example from industry. *BSI News*, October.
38. Garvin, D. A. (1983) Quality on the line. *Harvard Bus. Rev.*, September/October, 65–75.
39. Burns, C. R. (1976) Quality costing used as a tool for cost reduction in the machine tool industry. *Qual. Assur.*, **2**, (1), 25–32.
40. Webb, N. B. (1972) Auditing meat processor quality control costs. *Qual. Prog.*, February, 13–15.
41. Moyer, D. R. and Gilmore, H. L. (1979) Product conformance in the steel foundry jobbing shop. *Qual. Prog.*, May, 17–19.
42. Huckett, J. D. (1985) An outline of the quality improvement process at Rank Xerox. *Int. J. Qual. Reliab. Manage.*, **2** (2), 5–14.
43. Krzikowski, K. (1963) Quality control and quality costs within the mechanical industry, *Proc. 7th EOQC Conf. Copenhagen, September*, pp. 42–8.
44. Kohl, W. F. (1976) Hitting quality costs where they live. *Qual. Assur.*, **2**, (2), 59–64.
45. Jorgensen, J. (1963) Utilising quality cost information, *Proc. 7th EOCQ Conf., Copenhagen, September*, pp. 49–59.
46. Brown, A. C. (1973) Budgeting for the determined standard. *Qual. Eng.*, **37** (3), 73–75.
47. Mandel, B. J. (1972) Quality costing systems. *Qual. Prog.*, December, 11–13.
48. Olson, R. (1982) Putting Q.C. into good form. *Qual. Prog.*, January, 35–7.
49. Hallum, S. and Casperson, R. (1975). Economy and quality control, *Proc. 19th EOQC Conf., Venice*, pp. 11–22.
50. Cox, B. (1979) Interface of quality costing and terotechnology. *The Accountant*, 21 June, 800–1.
51. Cox B. (1982) The role of the management accountant in quality costing. *Qual. Assur.*, **8**, (3), 82–4.
52. Sandretto, M. J. (1985) What kind of a cost system do you need? *Harvard Bus. Rev.*, January/February, 110–18.

2
Definitions of quality costs

2.1 The importance of definitions

In any cost collection exercise the costs must be relevant to the topic. Therefore the importance of definitions to the collection, analysis and use of quality costs cannot be overstressed. Without clear definitions there can be no common understanding or meaningful communication on the topic of quality costing. The definition of what constitutes quality costs is by no means straightforward and there are many grey areas where good production/operations practices overlap with quality-related activities. Unfortunately there is no general agreement on a single broad definition of quality costs.

Quality costs may be regarded as one criterion of an organization's quality performance – but only if valid comparisons can be made between different sets of cost data. Clearly the comparability of sets of data is dependent on the definitions of the cost categories and elements used in compiling them. If definitions are not established and accepted, the only alternative would be to qualify every item of data so that at least it might be understood, even though it may not be comparable with other data. However, it is difficult to find generic terms to describe specific tasks or activities having the same broad objectives in different industries, organizations or types of manufacture and services. This makes collation and comparisons of data from different sources very difficult. Consequently, the value of much of the published quantitative data on quality-related costs may be questionable because of the absence of precise definitions and lack of qualification.

In view of this it is surprising that many practitioners and writers on quality costs appear to have been reluctant to get to grips with the problem of definitions *per se*. A number of definitions of quality-related costs are in fairly specious terms. Many authors avoid the issue altogether, though some have at least faced up to it before neatly side-stepping it. Some cost collectors and authors state or imply their definitions of quality-related costs. In other cases it is evident from the text, figures and/or discussions that the cost collector's view of what constitutes a quality-related cost is at odds with commonly accepted views. But despite obvious differences in interpretation, definitions of what constitutes quality costs are not discussed *per se*. Accountants are similarly not very forthcoming with definitions of costs which make clear how, for example, overheads should be dealt with or how scrap should be costed and this adds to the problem. Admittedly there are difficulties in preparing unambiguous acceptable definitions and it is understandable that most people writing on the subject avoid the issues, though the reluctance of the ASQC to define quality costs (other than by category and element) and the absence of definitions of 'total quality costs' in BS 4778: Part 1 (ISO 8402) *Quality Vocabulary* [1] despite its frequent use in BS 6413 [2] are curious omissions. However, in Part 2 of the revision of BS 6143 [3] quality-related costs are defined as 'cost in ensuring and assuring quality as well as loss incurred when quality is not achieved'.

It is interesting to report that overambition or overzealousness may prompt quality assurance specialists to try to maximize the impact of quality costs on the Chief Executive Officer and members of the senior management team; the same applies to Management Consultants. Consequently they tend to stretch their definitions to include those costs which have only the most tenuous relationship with the quality of the product and service. This is not necessarily for self-aggrandizement, but to try to create a financial impact. The problem with this attempt to amplify quality-related costs is that it can backfire. Once costs have been accepted as being quality related, the quality assurance manager may have some difficulty in exerting an influence over the reduction of costs which are independent of quality considerations. It is not always easy to disown costs after one has claimed them, especially if ownership is in a 'grey area' and no one else wants them.

The point being made here is that the question of definitions which is fundamental to the whole exercise of gathering and using quality-related costs is, in general, not given sufficient thought. Attention to definitions may obviate many of the obstacles to establishing quality costing as a management tool, for as the eminent philosophers Aristotle and Socrates respectively have observed:

> How many a dispute could have been deflated into a single paragraph if the disputants had dared define their terms.

and

The beginning of wisdom is the definition of terms.

2.2 Quality cost categories

A most striking feature of the literature is a preoccupation with the prevention–appraisal–failure (PAF) categorization. This is also the case when organizations categorize their quality costs. There can be little doubt that the prime reason for this is its adoption by the ASQC and subsequent incorporation into what is still, perhaps, the most definitive work on the subject, *Quality Costs – What and How* [4]. Subsequent adoption of this approach by various writers and the British Standards Institution (BSI) [1–3, 5] has resulted in it becoming very firmly entrenched in the current wisdom on quality costing. So much so that, although it was devised to deal with manufacturing industries, attempts have been made to apply its principles directly to other quite different industries. Aubrey and Zimbler [6], for example, claim to have successfully applied the approach in banking, Webb [7] has applied it to meat processing, and Ball [8] may be only a step away from using it when he looks at how the basic tenets of industrial quality assurance can be applied to hospital quality assurance. The PAF method has also been used in more recent times by British Airways Technical Workshops, National Westminster Bank and Hilti (Great Britain) Ltd in their marketing and service operations.

It should be noted that the arrangement of cost elements into the categories of prevention, appraisal and failure tends to be a post-collection exercise carried out to accord with convention. Categorization of costs in this way seems to be of greater interest to quality assurance managers than to anyone else in the business and perhaps a corollary of this approach is the preoccupation with in-house quality-related costs, with little specific attention being paid to supplier- or subcontractor-generated quality costs or to customer-related costs.

The widespread use and deep entrenchment of the PAF categorization of quality costs invites analysis of the reasons for it. This categorization is usually done after the collection exercise for reporting purposes and adds nothing to the data's potential for provoking action. It may facilitate comparison with earlier data from the same source, but even this may not be valid because of the dissimilarity between current warranty and guarantee costs, where these are applicable and/or included, to other current costs. The PAF categorization of costs is of interest and some value to quality assurance managers, but less so to other functional managers on the grounds that they do not relate directly to the activities of the business. However, there are some general and specific advantages to be gained from this type of categorization. Among the general advantages are that it may prompt a rational approach to collecting costs, and it can add orderliness and uniformity to the ensuing reports. Among the specific advantages of this particular categorization are, firstly, its universal acceptance; secondly, its conference of relative desirability of different kinds of expenditure; thirdly, and most importantly, it provides keyword criteria to help to decide whether costs are, in fact, quality related. The last-mentioned point may explain why neither Feigenbaum, the originator of the categorization, nor the ASQC, defines the term 'quality costs'. Matters are judged to be quality related if they satisfy the criteria set by their definitions of prevention, appraisal and failure.

There are alternatives to the PAF approach which are different but do not necessarily conflict with it because they are the same costs being collected under different headings. Chief among these alternatives (or supplementary) categorizations is division of costs into direct and indirect, controllable and uncontrollable, discretionary and consequential costs. Moyes and Rogerson [9] have devised classifications such that, in an industry where quality-related costs may account for up to one-third of the project cost, the main items of cost were found to arise from only four topics, namely validation inspection, special procedures, repair and rectification, and quality engineering.

Another approach is to consider the activities relating to supplier, company and customer. This idea came from the authors' observing quality assurance departments at work and the realization that the PAF concept of quality activities, for all its virtue, relates more to historical reporting of costs than to the activities of the company. It is suggested that costs categorized under 'supplier', 'company' and 'customer' headings would relate closely to the way companies work. This categorization applies to both manufacturing and service organizations. Quality costs categorized in this way would relate better to other business costs and would be easier for people to identify with. However, both the business and the quality concepts of costing could be met by the simple expedient of a supplier–company–customer versus prevention–appraisal–failure matrix, as illustrated in Figure 2.1. (The figure also indicates some of the major cost elements which might be included in the matrix.) This proposal has the merit of new categories which closely match the business activity whilst retaining the advantages of the established categorizaton. Further reference to alternative approaches are made in Chapters 3 and 5 on the collection and use of quality costs respectively. However, in the absence of a suitable broad definition of quality-related costs, definitions of prevention, appraisal and failure costs are good criteria for deciding whether or not particular costs are quality related.

	Supplier/Subcontractor	In-house	Customer
Prevention	SQA, feedback, advice, training Vendor assessment rating, and development Certification and accreditation Develop alternative sourcing plans Audits and site inspection Joint quality planning	Training Statistical process control Quality improvement teams Quality engineering Quality planning Design of experiments	Joint quality planning Field trials Evaluation of customer's packing, handling and storage arrangements Market research Customer audits and inspections
Appraisal	Incoming inspection Sorting Organizing returns and replacements Inspections at supplier's site Material certification/traceability	Inspection and test Product testing Calibration Checking procedures	Product sign-off/certification Liaise with customer inspection activity
Internal failure	Work costs to point of scrapping Rework costs Negotiate rework/sort prices Machining defective materials Lost production and disruption owing to defective material Negotiate reimbursements	Isolation of causes of failures Reinspection Modifications and concessions Scrap and associated costs Rework and associated costs Downgrading	Discount on goods accepted on concession Downgraded goods sold cheaply
External failure	Costs attributable to but not recoverable from supplier Complaint handling Receipt and disposal of defective goods	Analysis and correlation of feedback data	Complaint handling Customer returns Free-of-charge replacements Field repairs
Warranty	Costs attributable to suppliers but not recoverable	Analysis and correlation of feedback data	Warranty payments Warranty claim checking and negotiation
Other	Excess stocks to buffer delivery failures Preparation of specifications	Records of quality-related activities Quality performance reporting Quality costing Interdisciplinary quality task groups	Product liability provision/insurance

Figure 2.1 Quality cost matrix.

Inevitably there are examples of disagreement to be found of what is included under the cost categories of prevention, appraisal and failure and even the BSI and the ASQC differ in their categorization of two minor cost elements. However, there is general acceptance and common understanding of the nature of costs in these categories, despite some ambiguities and differences in wording which occur, for example, between the BSI and ASQC publications. The ambiguity arises in the definitions of external failure costs where despite differences in wording both authorities leave the door open to admit for inclusion all sorts of costs (including, for example, fair wear and tear and forfeited goodwill) for an indefinite period. Many of the post-sales costs and post-warranty costs which could be included under this category, as defined, would not normally be incurred by manufacturers and providers of services. As to differences in wording, it is clear that the intent is the same in both cases, but it is curious that BSI have amended the definitions of the categories without making appropriate adjustments to the definitions of the elements in the categories. Thus, for example, the ASQC definition of prevention costs:

> costs incurred for planning, implementing and maintaining a quality system that will assure conformance to quality requirements at economic levels

has been amended by BSI in BS 6143 (1981) [2] to:

> the costs of any action taken to investigate, prevent or reduce defects and failures

and in BS 6143: Part 2 (1990) [3] to:

> these costs are incurred to reduce failure and appraisal costs to a minimum.

However, BSI's definition of prevention elements remains very much in line with the ASQC definition of elements.

2.3 Quality cost elements

Within each cost category there are many cost elements from which the total quality cost may be synthesized. BS 6143: Part 2 [3] and the ASQC publication *Quality Costs – What and How* [4] identify a list of cost elements under the cost categories of prevention, appraisal, internal failure and external failure. These lists act as a guideline for the purpose of quality cost collection. Some of the elements listed are not relevant to particular industries and service-related organizations. On the other hand, many elements identified by practitioners are peculiar to an industry – service and manufacturing or even a manufacturing unit sector or situation; such elements, by their definition, are not identified in either of these publications. Some writers (e.g. Oseberg [10] point out that individual cost definitions relevant to the company organization, types of products, number of products, and the degree of controlled processes, or automation, need to be established. Papers by Burns [11] from the machine-tool industry, Garvin [12] writing about air-conditioning equipment manufacture, Grant and Rogerson [13] from the process plant industry, Schmidt and Jackson [14] on diesel engine manufacture, Brown [15] and Abed and Dale [16] on the manufacture of textiles, and Blank and Solorzano [17] and Groocock (e.g. [18]) on electrical/electronic manufacture all make it clear that each case is different. With the developing interest by commerce, the public sector and service organizations in the concept of quality costing this is likely, in the near future, to identify a number of 'new' cost elements.

Business situations may also play a part in what might be included in quality cost elements. Burns [11], for example, lists intangibles which include loss of reputation and goodwill, whilst for others additional capital requirements imposed by the pursuit of quality improvement may be of prime importance, as reported by Besterfield [19] and Kirkpatrick [20]. Brewer [21] includes pilferage losses, sales and marketing operations ('costs attributable to overstaffing and related expenses resulting from inflated sales projections; sales and marketing costs associated with defect complaints, investigations and soothing irate customers; excessive promotional or advertising expenses to market low-quality products'), expenses attributable to financial management, industrial relations and materials procurement causes. Mertz [22] too points the finger at sales staff dealing wth problems instead of selling, and at financing additional inventory to cover for scrapped work. Witts [23] from the car industry gives a comprehensive picture of the inputs to product quality (and hence cost) from design through to warranty control – and identifies areas for improvement in all of them. Garvin [12] also provides food for thought on sources of quality costs when he discusses them under programmes, policies and attitudes, information systems, product design, production and work force policies, and vendor management. In one case encountered by the authors, the quality assurance manager included stock losses in his quality costing reports. He contended that much of the material which gets lost is non-conforming work which is deliberately obscured by operators.

A cost element which many contributors to the literature list without comment is 'lost opportunity cost'. It occurs so frequently that one might expect to find it and its constituent elements defined and discussed at some length. It is not so. Most people have ideas about how they may be incurred and in broad terms what they are, but there is great reticence about quantifying them, though the general inference is that they must be huge. The Institution of Cost and Management Accounting (ICMA) does not have a formal definition of 'lost opportunity cost' among its official terminology. Nor do business and management dictionaries define it. In the authors' view the sum total of an organization's 'lost opportunity cost' can only amount to the difference in profit accruing from their current output and the output they might reasonably aspire to. Given the swings and roundabouts of trade, the lost opportunity cost of a single failure is probably relatively small.

2.4 Difficulties associated with quality cost definitions

It must be appreciated that problems of rigorous definitions arise only because of the desire to carry out a quality costing exercise. Consideration of quality in other contexts (e.g. education and training, supply and storage, design, document and engineering changes, and statistical process control) does not require such sharp distinction to be made between what is quality related and what is not. But there is ample evidence to show that, even when collecting costs, collectors do not feel constrained to stick to rigorously defined elements. By and large collectors devise their own elements to suit their own industry, commercial or service situation, within the framework of the widely accepted PAF categorization. The result is a proliferation of uniquely defined cost elements which preclude comparison of data from different sources. Fortunately there have been few attempts and no success in proliferating categories of costs. There is little doubt that, in general, proliferation of categories and elements adds to the difficulties of cost definitions and limits the broad uses of quality costs. As well as being undesirable it may also be unnecessary.

Two of the salient points which are important to any discussion of quality costing are that accounting systems do not readily yield the information needed, as it is presently defined, and that rigorous definitions of quality activity elements are necessary only for costing purposes. Thus there is an apparently absurd situation of defining elements in a way which makes them difficult to cost. Elements are usually identified from specific activities or expenditures arising from product and/or service non-conformance (in the broadest sense) without much consideration of the ease of costing. Given that accounting systems are unlikely to change radically to accommodate quality costing difficulties, there should be greater consideration of the accounting aspects when defining quality cost elements. The objective must be to redefine cost quality elements to align with the business activities of the company, and fit in with the costing structure. Warranty cost is an example of such an element. It is clearly quality related, it is part of the business agreement between a company and its customers, and a company must make financial provisions to meet its liabilities. Another example is the quality costing situation encountered in some companies in which most of the data come directly from cost centres or labour-booking accounts.

When considering definitions of quality and their susceptibility to costing, the accountant's preference for definitions which are constrained to meeting specification has much to commend it. Open-ended definitions such as the definition of quality as 'fitness for purpose', whilst it is commendable and easy to say, admits too many intangibles and makes quality costing more difficult. If, say, 'fitness for purpose' is the quality objective it must be met through suitable specifications and measures of customer needs and expectations. The cost collectors must not be left in the difficult situation of trying to decide what parameters affect the product's and/or service's suitability for its purpose.

There are differing views between the quality fraternity and the accounting fraternity of what product and service quality is about and hence the cost of quality. It is interesting to observe that accountants appear to be uncompromising in their insistence that, for the purposes of quality costing, the definition of quality needs to be constrained or qualified by bringing 'meeting specification' into their definitions. Whilst the correctness of this may be debatable, it is understandable that accountants (who, after all, are likely to be charged with the responsibility of putting costs on the identified cost elements) do not want open-ended definitions adding to their problems. The difficulties which accountants face in gathering quality costs stem not only from a lack of agreement on definitions of quality and related activities but also because considerations of quality bring in parameters not usually noted or measured in management accounting reporting. Furthermore, there is a lack of definitions of quality-related costs in purely accounting terms. The only quality definitions in the ICMA's official terminology are of quality costs and quality cost variance. The profession could do the quality fraternity and themselves a service if it pronounced judgements on a few of the major issues such as allocation of overheads and valuation of scrapped goods and materials.

The problem of whether or not testing and running-in-type activities involving some adjustment of the product are a quality cost arises at most of the companies which have been studied by the authors. Carson [24] is positive that testing is about detecting defects, that it is an appraisal cost, and that there is an onus on the manufacturing/operations department to 'get it right first time.' Testing is effectively proving the 'fitness for purpose' of the product and/or service in one or more respects. There may well be cases where such testing ought not to be necessary, but is, and hence incurs a quality cost. However, in many cases the state of the technology may be such that testing is unavoidable. An organization may be unable to give guarantees to their customers without testing the product. They may be unable to get insurance cover without testing. In the end, the decision whether to test or not may be taken out of their hands, irrespective of whatever they think they can achieve without testing. In such circumstances should testing be regarded as a quality cost or purely a production operations activity? And if it is treated as a quality cost, is it an appraisal or a prevention cost? Because each case is different it is not possible to offer a general solution to this problem other than to suggest that if there is serious doubt, the cost should not be defined as being quality related where it is unlikely to be amenable to change by quality management influences. Other suggested criteria are that an item is quality related when: (1) if less is spent on it, failure costs increase; and (2) if more is spent on it, failure costs decrease.

Similar problems of categorization arise for costs generated by functions other than quality assurance and production/operations. Notable examples are the contributions of the purchasing function to supplier quality assurance and assistance and in ensuring the fitness for purpose of purchased goods, and the activities of engineering and design departments involved with concessions and design modifications prompted by product quality considerations. Quantifying, classifying and costing such inputs are very difficult and are seldom done, but they can amount to significant proportions of the prevention and internal failure expenditure categories respectively.

There are those factors which serve to ensure the basic utility of the product, guard against errors, and protect and preserve product and service quality. Examples are the use of design codes, preparation of engineering and administrative systems and procedures, capital premiums on machinery, document and drawing controls, and handling and storage practices. Whether such factors give rise to costs which may be regarded as being quality related is a matter for judgement in individual cases.

There is also the question of whether quality-related costs should include a portion of the costs of site services such as catering, security, etc. The consensus opinion is that they should not, but some practitioners feel that the full costs of quality are not being measured if some such allocation for this activity is not made.

Obviously such problems need to be discussed with purchasing, engineering, production/operations, and accountancy personnel, as appropriate, in order to resolve them. It is unlikely, however, that there will be a uniform view, and it is improbable that the prevailing accounting practices will yield ready-made or satisfactory solutions.

An aspect of definitions which is worth discussing briefly is the sensitivity of costs to changes in product and service quality. It was noted at one company studied that despite dramatic improvements in product quality there was little evidence of corresponding changes in quality costs. The matter arose again in a different form at another company where they were looking for a cost reporting system which reflected quality performance. Unfortunately there are many costs which do not change in line with quality improvement. These costs are often large and obscure those costs which do change with quality improvement initiatives. The answer to the problem seems to be to identify and isolate those parts of the cost which change (or will ultimately change) in relation to the quality improvement and to report them separately, perhaps as projected savings, if necessary.

2.5 Concessions, modifications and engineering changes

To anyone investigating costs in manufacturing industry, striking features are (1) the large amount of time and money spent on modifications and engineering changes, and (2) an apparent acceptance, in particular amongst design, engineerng and technical personnel, that they are facts of organizational life that one must learn to live with; one gets the feeling that this is the way organizations go about their respective businesses. It is important to reflect that the main reason there are so many problematic engineering changes is that the design was often a problem to begin with. If products were designed right the first time using design for manufacture concepts, quality function deployment, failure mode and effects analysis (FMEA), etc., these types of changes would be kept to a minimum. Thus they might justifiably be categorized as in-built costs. The costs, though hidden, are believed by the authors to be substantial and, quite apart from the costs of personnel directly involved, there can be serious implications for inventory levels and even impediments to output if modifications and changes are not kept to a minimum. It is also important to ensure that the processing of the modifications and changes does not become protracted.

There is a need for a new set of definitions to help determine the cost associated with concessions and engineering changes. In the authors' experience these are major quality activities but little is known about the cost. It is necessary also to focus attention on these activities to make people more aware of them, and to make accountable those people who are responsible for the costs. It is not simply good enough just to budget monies to cater for concessions and engineering changes.

It is suspected that in many companies concessions are an expedient way of maintaining production schedules and that little account is taken of the disadvantages incurred in deciding to overlook non-conformances. Not least among these are the proliferation of paperwork and engendering lax attitudes towards quality improvement among managers, supervisors and shopfloor workers. In fact, frequent concessions on non-conforming goods are a positive disincentive to operators to get operations right the first time.

In many companies goods passed on concession do not feature in quality reporting systems because they have escaped the company's non-conformance reporting. In some companies goods are supposed only to be passed on concession if they cannot be rectified. It is often easier to find reasons why goods cannot be rectified than it is to rework them. Hence concession systems may become an engineering expediency, or, equally, they may become a production expediency to avoid impediments to output or delays in delivery. All in all it is felt that the quality cost implications of concessions granted on non-conforming goods are probably far greater than can be inferred from the literature on quality costs and discussions on the subject and that many of the associated costs may never be picked up using conventional quality costs' checklists and guidelines.

There can be no doubt that between concessions, modifications and engineering changes there is a sizeable quality-related activity escaping the quality cost net at most organizations. The prime reason why these costs may not be identified and picked up is because they do not feature in quality non-conformance reports. There is a clear need for additional cost elements to be defined identifying the kinds of quality-related costs which arise from concessions, modifications and engineering changes.

References

1. BS 4778: Part 1 (1987) *Quality Vocabulary International Terms*, British Standards Institution, London.
2. BS 6143 (1981) *The Determination and Use of Quality-Related Costs*, British Standards Institution, London.
3. BS 6143: Part 2 (1990) *The Guide to the Economics of Quality: Prevention, appraisal and failure model*, British Standards Institution, London.
4. ASQC Quality Costs Committee (1970) *Quality Costs – What and How*, American Society for Quality Control, Milwaukee, WI.
5. BS 4981 (1972) *A Guide to Quality Assurance*, British Standards Institution, London.
6. Aubrey, C. A. II and Zimbler, D. A. (1983) Quality costs and improvements. *Qual. Prog.*, 16–20.
7. Webb, N. B. (1972) Auditing meat processing quality control costs. *Qual. Prog.*, February, 13–15.
8. Ball, L. W. (1984) The relevance of industrial quality assurance to hospital quality assurance. *Qual. Assur.*, **10**, (3), 84–7.
9. Moyes, E. M. and Rogerson, J. H. (1983) *The Reduction of Quality-Related Costs in the Process Plant Industry*, Process Plant EDC.

10. Oseberg, M. (1963) Acquiring quality cost information, *Proc. 7th EOQC Conf., Copenhagen*, pp. 25–30.

11. Burns, C. R. (1976) Quality costing used as a tool for cost reduction in the machine tool industry. *Qual. Assur.*, **2**, (1), 25–32.

12. Garvin, D. A. (1983) Quality on the line. *Harvard Bus. Rev.*, September/October, 65–75.

13. Grant, I. M. and Robertson, J. H. (1981) The importance of contractual requirements in determining quality costs in the fabrication industry, *Proc. Welding Institute Conf., London*.

14. Schmidt, J. W. and Jackson, J. F. (1982) Measuring the cost of product quality. *Automot. Eng. (Warrendale, PA)*, **90**, (6), 42–8.

15. Brown, A. C. (1973) Budgeting for the determined standard. *Qual. Eng.*, **37**, (3), 73–5.

16. Abed, A. H. and Dale, B. G. (1987) An attempt to identify quality-related costs in textile manufacturing. *Qual. Assur.*, **13**, (2), 41–5.

17. Blank, L. and Solorzano, J. (1978) Using quality cost analysis for management improvements. *Ind. Eng.*, **10**, (2), 46–51.

18. Groocock, J. M. (1975) ITT Europe's quality cost improvement programme. *Qual. Assur.*, **2**, (2), 35–40.

19. Besterfield, B. M. (1979) *Quality Control*, Prentice-Hall, Englewood Cliffs, NJ.

20. Kirkpatrick, E. G. (1970) *Quality Control for Managers and Engineers*, Wiley, Sussex.

21. Brewer, C. W. (1978) Zero based profit assurance. *Qual. Prog.*, 15–27.

22. Mertz, O. R. (1977) Quality's role in ROI. *Qual. Prog.*, 14–18.

23. Witts, M. T. (1976) Participation in industry. *Qual. Eng.*, **33**, (3), 3–7.

24. Carson, J. K. (1986) Quality costing – a practical approach. *Int. J. Qual. Reliab. Manage.*, **3**, (1), 54–63.

3

Collection of quality costs

3.1 Establishing the objectives for quality cost collection

There is little point in collecting quality costs just to see what they may reveal. Many managers have successfully resisted pressure to cooperate in the collection of costs on the grounds that cost would not reveal any problems of which they were not already aware from the organization's existing quality management information system. Thus, the effect of the quality costing strategy on the measurement and collection of quality costs is a key issue. Whilst Leibert [1] and Jenney [2] stress the importance of clear and concise objectives, there has been little comment in the literature on the significance of this. There is little doubt that getting the purposes of the exercise clear at the outset can have a considerable influence on the strategy; it is also of significant importance to the success of the project. For example, if the main purpose of the exercise is to identify high-cost problems, coarse-scale costs in known problem areas will suffice. If, on the other hand, the purpose is to set a percentage cost-reduction target on the company's total quality-related costs, it will be necessary to identify and measure all the contributing cost elements in order to be sure that costs are reduced and not simply transferred elsewhere. Thus, the matter is important, not only from a philosophical point of view, but from purely practical considerations as well.

The reason for failure to discuss in the literature the implications of differing objectives may be that almost all contributors favour the approach which identifies specific quality cost improvement projects. This approach initially requires only approximate costs (with which to identify and rank projects and, later, more precise costs, but in a narrow field of activity and cost) to be measured. The universality of this approach is matched only by the prevention–appraisal–failure categorization of cost and it is largely due to Juran's influence.

Instances of quality management practitioners favouring the Juran [3, 4] approach are too numerous to mention. His advocacy of 'quick and dirty' estimates to identify quality improvement projects worth tackling has an immense attraction for the busy manager, though one wonders how quick and dirty an estimate of ±15% which he uses by way of example may really be. But when faced with his alternative of restructuring the accounting system in order to evaluate accurately total quality costs, the project approach becomes doubly attractive.

It is worth noting that those contributors who give an overview of measurement and collection of quality costs take a circumspect view of the topic. For example, Jenney [2] stresses that minimizing quality costs is not the only criterion. Many authors make the point that accuracy is not at a premium and warn not to expect too much from the first attempt at quality costing.

Therefore, possible quality costing strategies range from measuring and monitoring all quality costs to costing only specific quality improvement projects and activities. An organization's total quality costs inevitably include large immutable costs and the powerful arguments which are put forward for measuring only costs which change tend to erode the case for collecting total quality costs. It is typically argued that there is little point in gathering and presenting, on a routine basis, costs which do not change. Consequently, before setting up a quality cost collection system, it is advisable to examine the potential for change of a cost element in both absolute and relative terms. The inclusion of fixed or immutable costs also has the effect of reducing the sensitivity of costs to performance-improving changes. On the other hand, if costs are not being monitored, how does one know that they are not going to change? An acceptable compromise is to carry out occasional total cost exercises but to monitor regularly and emphasize only those costs which are likely to change with improvement activities. The basis of the argument supporting this view is that it is unnecessary to know all the costs to be sure, for example, that quality costs are decreasing.

Another argument, leading to a similar conclusion, is that if a company is looking to reduce costs while improving product and service quality (or vice versa), it needs some measures of quality and cost performance, and of their relationship to each other. Further, it needs only quality maintenance costs and those costs which can or do change with quality. Whilst such arguments are plausible and superficially attractive, they imply that some key costs are sensitive to quality changes and that the relationship is known and understood. In reality, this is far from being the case. The authors firmly believe that it is important to know the total quality-related costs, including those which do not change, so that the effects of changes in elemental costs on total costs may be seen. The classic and often-quoted example of failure to do this is that of reducing inspection costs only to increase failure costs by a far greater amount.

One of the important decisions on quality costing strategy, to be taken at the outset, concerns the assignment of accountability. Deciding in advance who should be accountable for what may produce a very different cost report to one based on the usual quality-based criteria. Also, on the subject of accountability, the production function is the most closely measured and accountable group in manufacturing organizations. Hence, it is usual for cost collecting to start there. It is important to make sure it does not end there, for although the manufacturing function has a prime responsibility for quality, there are many other departments in a company who contribute to product and service quality, to failure and to quality costs. The technique of departmental purpose analysis (DPA) or departmental improvement review (DIR) is a useful means of getting quality performance measurements and quality improvement activities accepted in non-manufacturing departments and areas; the technique of DIR is described by Payne in Dale and Plunkett [5].

When actually collecting quality costs it is sometimes easy to lose sight of the fact that the task is primarily a cost collection exercise, and that cost collection exercises have other, different, criteria which are sensibly independent of the cost topic. Suitable criteria include purpose, relevance, ease of collection, size, accuracy, completeness, potential for change, recording and presentation, and uses. A set of back-up criteria like these, which are independent of the cost topic, can often provide useful ways out of the dilemma about whether or not particular activities and costs should be included in a costing exercise. They will ensure that the data which are collected are understood and can be qualified. In the authors' experience the collection and synthesis of quality costs is very much a matter of searching and shifting through data which have been gathered for other purposes.

3.2 Available advice on quality cost collection

The aspect of measuring and collecting quality cost, though obviously central to a quality cost reduction exercise, is poorly covered by most contributors to the literature. The cost collecting exercise can, of itself, and irrespective of the topic, present all sorts of difficulties. Perhaps this is why even the most eminent writers appear to skip over the subject.

Many papers touch on it but give little help and guidance to the practitioner setting out to gather quality costs. There is a lack of detailed guidance from accountants and some leading quality management consultants appear to have side-stepped the problem in their general advocacy of the establishment and use of quality costing. In the case of the latter, they often oversimplify the difficulties encountered in quality cost collection. They typically argue that much of the cost data are readily available and that data can be collected in a few days. Many writers on the subject confine themselves to why and what to collect and some skip lightly on to presentation and use. It should be noted that the often optimistic expectations of the quality fraternity are counterbalanced by the more cautious outlook of the accountants who are expected to do the work.

A brief survey of the accounting literature uncovered little guidance on cost collection exercises in general. It might be imagined that such a common exercise would have generated a considerable body of literature setting down criteria and advising on allocation of overheads, avoiding double counting, etc. Not so. Perhaps accountants feel that such matters are too elementary to be worth writing down or that it is unnecessary to give guidance to non-accountants, presumably in the belief that collecting costs is really an accountant's job and that their professional training equips them to deal with the problems which arise. Nevertheless, non-accountants frequently become involved in cost collecting exercises and some informal guidance would surely be welcomed by would-be collectors.

However, a select band of contributors do give guidance on how to do it and show some appreciation of the practicalities likely to be encountered in the exercise. It should not be forgotten that any project which crosses departmental boundaries and functions is almost bound to run into more difficulties than projects contained within a single department. Accounting systems are not usually set up in such a way that cost collection exercises which cross conventional boundaries can easily be made.

The merits and demerits of the ASQC publication and the British Standard have already been discussed at some length in the earlier chapters of this book. However, they both recommend a pilot study approach, principally, perhaps out of recognition and/or department needs to develop their own detailed procedures and systems within the framework outlined in these publications.

Some authors advocate starting the cost collection exercise by looking at internal failure costs. Feigenbaum [6] reflects a mini-version of the ASQC publication *What and How* (which in turn is based on the 1961 edition of his book *Total Quality Control*). Hallum and Casperson [7] show how straightforward cost collection can be, given a cost accounting system which appears to be purpose designed for cost collection exercises which cut across departmental and other cost boundaries. Blank and Solozarno [8], Booth [9] and Alford [10–12] all clearly have first-hand experience of collecting quality costs and it shows in their thoroughly practical papers on the subject.

3.3 Various approaches to quality cost collection

There are a variety of ways in which organizations can go about collecting and measuring quality costs. A summary of the most popular methods is now given.

The list of cost elements identified in publications such as BS 6143 [13] and the ASQC's *Quality Costs: What and How* [14] is a useful guideline. A variation on this method is for the cost collector to analyse the quality costing literature (including these two publications) and identify, from what has been written about the subject, potential elements of cost which are relevant to their organization. These methods are mainly used in cases where the organization is engaged in the manufacture of mechanical and electrical products.

In other manufacturing environments such as paint, chemicals, rubber and textiles, the list of elements which are readily available from the literature and BS 6143 [13] and ASQC [14], are not necessarily applicable in these cases. Hence the cost collector, while using such lists as a useful starting point, will be required to develop their own list of cost elements from company-specific experience.

In the view of the authors, it is not practical to compile an all-embracing list of quality cost elements to cover all eventualities as attempted in BS 6143 [13] and ASQC [14], as there will always be those which are specific to particular situations and industries. The way forward may be for each industry sector to compile its own list of cost elements. The main purpose of the list of elements given in BS 6143 and the ASQC publications is to facilitate quality cost comparison between companies. However, as already pointed out, such comparisons are both dangerous and fraught with difficulties. Consequently, the main use of the list of elements is to act as thought promoters and mind openers and to demonstrate to senior managers the type of quality costs their organizations are likely to be incurring. However, using a list of published cost elements to identify quality costs can also act as blinkers.

When the cost element method is used, the first step is to identify the elements of costs, the second is to quantify the elements and the final step is to cost the elements. The usual approach is for a quality assurance and or technical specialist, in conjunction with other appropriate company personnel, to take responsibility for identifying the elements and provide appropriate quantitative data relating to each element. The accountant will put costs on the elements which have been identified. It is helpful if the quality assurance and technical personnel liaise with the accountant during this activity.

In non-manufacturing situations, the cost elements described in BS 6143 [13] and the ASQC [14] publications and in the popular quality costing literature are often of little use to the cost collector. As with the case of non-engineering-type products, the cost collectors must strive to develop their own list of cost elements specific to their situation. The following two semi-structured methods are of value in helping to develop a list of quality cost elements. It should be noted that these methods can also be employed in a manufacturing environment.

Method

1. After an introduction by the Chief Executive Officer, confirming their commitment to quality costing as an essential aspect of TQM, a quality assurance/technical specialist will give a briefing on the concept of quality costing to all departmental heads and members of the senior management team. The briefing typically includes what are quality costs, their uses, the concept of cost categories and elements, examples of specific cost elements in the organization, why the organization is setting out to identify quality costs, and the methodology which is to be employed to identify, collect and measure the costs. As part of this briefing, some organizations use a questionnaire relating to the various activities of the organization in order to help people distinguish quality parameters into types of prevention, appraisal and failure activities. This assists in developing a common understanding within the organization of the three types of cost categories.

The managers are given a briefing pack on quality costs and are requested to make the same presentation on quality costs to their staff and explain the quality costing methodology to them. It should be noted that some organizations take the view that in the initial stages of the quality costing exercise, the emphasis is on just identifying the costs of failure and appraisal activities. The methodology is for each department (e.g. marketing, personnel, purchasing and finance), using a team approach, to identify elements of quality costs which are appropriate to them and for which they have ownership. The Quality Management tools and techniques, such as brainstorming, cause and effect analysis, forcefield analysis and why diagrams, are useful aids to facilitate quality cost element identification.

Once the elements have been identified, the departmental heads make a presentation to the technical and or quality assurance specialists. The presentations made and the relevant synergy which develops during the discussion help to refine each department's list of cost elements.

After the elements have been agreed the next step is for each depart-

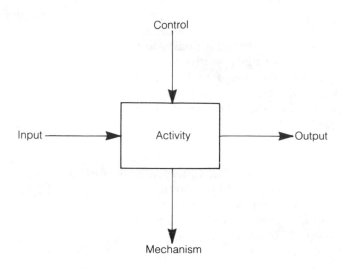

Figure 3.1 IDEF – The ICOM code.

ment to determine the amount of time they are spending on each cost element which has been identified. During this activity the cost of wastage on items such as paper, materials, forms, etc., is also identified. The quality assurance and technical specialists assist the departments in the task. The accountant then works with each departmental manager and with the technical and quality assurance specialists, as appropriate, in putting a cost on each element identified.

Method

2. Using the computer-aided manufacturing integrated program definition method (IDEF) (Ross *et al.* [15]) each department is treated as a process. This process modelling method (see Figure 3.1) was first used by for the identification of quality cost elements by Marsh [16]. The method employs an activity box with inputs, outputs, controls and mechanisms. The revised BS 6143 (Part 1) includes a process cost model [17] and detailed guidance is given in the Standard on the use of this method for quality costing The methodology focuses on departmental objectives and process ownership, and helps people to identify the costs of conformance and the costs of non-conformance which are associated with the processes for which they have responsibility. A model of each process is developed. This identifies all the parameters and activities within that process to be monitored and in which area of

the two costs they fall. The British Standards Institution is to be applauded for including this methodology in the revision of BS 6143. This will help to extend the concept of quality costing to all functions of an enterprise and to non-manufacturing organizations. It also gets people to consider in more detail the processes being carried out within their organization.

The IDEF methodology was developed for use by experts for the modelling of manufacturing systems. It is interesting to note that, after substantial research by Crossfield [18] in the modelling of quality system elements, the opinion was formed that if individuals were to take ownership for modelling their particular aspect of the quality system, a more simpler method was required. This led to the development of quality management activity planning (Q-MAP) for the mapping of quality assurance procedures, information, flows and quality-related responsibilities; see Crossfield and Dale [19]. Q-MAP has been used by a wide range of company personnel from shopfloor operators to members of the senior management team.

In discussions held by the authors with managers concerning the collection of quality costs using an IDEF type of approach there was almost universal agreement that if they and departmental staff were to be responsible for identifying the elements of costs, then perhaps the method was too complex. This was the same finding as that reached by Crossfield [18] in relation to quality system mapping. However, if a quality assurance/technical specialist or a quality management consultation is to take responsibility for the process modelling and identification of costs, then this method is appropriate.

It should be noted that whilst these two methods facilitate ownership of the costs by each department they sometimes fail to identify those costs which occur between departments. Consequently, some costs are not identified and even if they are, difficulties are encountered in persuading departmental managers to take responsibility for their ownership and subsequent reduction. It can also lead to departments attempting to minimize their costs at the expense of other departments, so ultimately the benefits to the organization as a whole are diminished. Cross-function cooperation is necessary if quality costing is to be a success and perhaps these latter two methods are not particularly apt in facilitating cooperation of this type.

3.4 Ease of collection

Most companies have materials and direct labour costs analysed in considerable details for the purpose of measuring production efficiencies. However, indirect labour (including staff personnel) costs are seldom analysed in detail even though they may total four or five times the direct labour costs. Thus, prevention is the most difficult of the categories to cost because it depends heavily on estimates of apportionment of time by indirect works and staff who do not usually record how they spend their day.

In those cases where indirect personnel are engaged on single activities or a narrow range of closely related activities (e.g. inspection), the cost is much easier to collect. In practice, however, many personnel are involved in a number of disparate activities, sometimes wholly quality related, sometimes not. It is the lack of data about how people spend their time which makes the collection of cost data under the different quality categories and elements difficult. In order to obtain a prevention cost synthesis it is necessary to record or estimate the proportions of time spent by various personnel on each activity. Retrospective estimates of the proportions of time spent on various activities tend to be highly subjective and are 'average' or 'typical' observations. In one organization studied by the authors, the quality assurance manager's perception of how his three quality engineers spent their time was wildly different from their own analysis. If such costs are to be collected on a routine basis it will be necessary for many staff to report on the use of their time. For personnel within the quality assurance department it is presumably within the quality assurance manager's authority to require routine accounting of staff time, weekly returns of half-day increments would suffice. The quality-related topics against which to book time, and personnel costs to be used in conjunction with such booking, are discussed later.

It should be noted that, in relation to prevention, some organizations take the view that this is a desirable cost and consequently they do not include it in their quality costing reporting system; they only collect and report the cost of failure and appraisal.

Some quality-related costs arising within the production function can be readily obtained from routine monthly accounts. Other quality activities such as sorting and inspection work undertaken by production personnel are not so easy to identify and cost. A cost which is not collected and which is very difficult to estimate with acceptable accuracy is the cost of personnel (other than quality assurance department personnel) whose work is partly generated as a result of failures. Examples are the involvement of purchasing and accounts personnel in dealing with supplier rejects, and production control personnel rescheduling rework in terms of components and batches of product. Analysis of failure costs by functional causes (e.g. production, purchasing, marketing) is another type of cost which is not usually readily available. Within manufacturing industry these are regarded as very important costs.

Another consideration in relation to ease of collection is the matter of labelling of account codes. It sometimes happens that accounts departments wish to keep separate accounts of some non-routine matter (e.g. a product recall) and give it a title from which it is not immediately obvious that it may be a quality cost. Hence it is prudent to work very closely with the accounts departments when investigating quality costs.

3.5 The level of detail in the costs collected

An obvious but often overlooked fact is that costing systems only trans-late other information into costs (i.e. the subject matter needs to be a matter of record before it can be picked up by a costing system). It follows that the potential for costing at a company may be gauged from the sophistication of their management information systems, and also that overambitious pursuit of detailed cost information will, of necess-ity, proliferate recording and analysis of underlying information.

Care must also be taken not to concentrate only on what is already known with a view to refining it. Size is often regarded as being synony-mous with importance, though it is size coupled with relevance and potential for reduction which determines the real importance of costs. Clearly, if refining costs is the object of the exercise, it is probably much more advantageous to refine known large costs than to quantify known sources of small costs. It is also better to pursue a small percentage reduction in a large cost than a large reduction in a small cost, depend-ing on the ease of achievement. What magnitude of cost may be regarded as being insignificant in the cost collection exercise is another problem. Unfortunately there are no useful guidelines, nor are ratios helpful, though accuracy levels, if known, may give good indications. In the end it becomes a subjective decision about what sum of money is significant in the context of quality costs or, perhaps, company profit. It is suggested that all costs which are readily available should be collected, but that cost elements which are likely to be less than £1000 per annum are not worth pursuing.

Having decided on a figure, it is important to recognize that it is much more likely that the magnitude of cost may fail to be picked up as part of a large cost element than of a small element. The strategy must therefore be to concentrate on the large-cost items.

It is important also to remember that the size of costs, both absolute and relative, can become grossly distorted under some accounting prac-tices. An example met with is the practice of including full overheads in direct labour charges to quality-related costs. Thus rework and scrap costs become grossly inflated compared with prevention and appraisal costs which are incurred via salaried and indirect workers. Such a system is, of course, not tenable in that there is some double-counting inevitably taking place. Another example of distortion is the influence of some countries' tax regulations on the valuation of scrap material.

It should also not be forgotten that if the quality costing system demands that information is collected on a regular basis in minute detail, there is a good chance that the system will fall into disuse. Considerable attention needs to be given to the number of cost elements to be collected and the sources of information.

3.6 Accuracy of data

Accuracy is one of the most important criteria in that it has a strong and direct influence on the amount of work involved in the task and on the credibility of the outcome. It is not usually practicable to decide in advance of the task the level of accuracy at which to work, or which is attainable. The precision is usually determined by factors outside the control of the quality cost investigator. A particularly apt piece of advice on the topic is contained in the following quotation:

> It is the mark of an instructed mind to rest content with that degree of precision which the nature of the subject permits and not to seek exactness where only approximation of the truth is possible.
>
> Aristotle

Because quality cost data are expressed in figures, which are sometimes treated by people as being very precise, there is a danger that cost reports may give an impression of accuracy which is not warranted. The true accuracy of costs is dependent on the underlying data. Knowledge of how these data are obtained and the purposes for which they are used may give good indications of the accuracy which may reasonably be sought or expected. Resorting to underlying data can also have the advantage that corroborative information may be available, though corresponding costs may not be. A case in point is failures under warranty encountered at one company studied by the authors.

The accuracy sought has a strong and direct influence on the amount of work involved in the task and on the credibility of the outcome. It is not usually practicable to decide in advance of the task the level of accuracy at which to work, or which is attainable. It is usually determined by factors outside the control of the cost investigator.

Accuracy of costs is dependent on the quality of underlying data. Knowledge of how those data are obtained and the purposes for which they are used may give good indications of the levels of accuracy which might reasonably be sought or expected. For example, in a situation where non-productive hours of direct workers are deducted from total hours before calculating labour and production efficiencies, there may be an incentive to carry out non-productive work (e.g. sorting of con-

forming from non-conforming product) inefficiently or even to misallo-
cate time at the expense of quality-related costs. Poor control of paperwork may also lead to inaccuracies. In-process rejection notes may
provide an example. Each note carries a unique number, but there may
be no system for checking that all notes issued are accounted for when
it comes to costing the various disposal outlets (scrap, rework, etc.). It
may be the case that a significant number of rejection notes which
ought to go to the quality assurance and accounts departments for
costing purposes never get there.

When trying to get a feel for the accuracy of cost information accumulated in accounts departments it is often useful to look for independent
measures as corroboration. In one company studied there appeared to
be inconsistencies between provision made for warranty claims, actual
warranty charges accumulated, product failure rate, and the level of
effort devoted to customer-rejected products and warranty investigations.

In apportioning personnel time to quality cost elements and categories, the use of actual costs, which may vary from month to month, may
not be warranted. Average rates based on annual employment costs
will be accurate enough. Nor is it necessary to have an employment
cost for every individual. Two or three levels of cost could give sufficient
accuracy. These figures may also provide useful checks in making inter-
divisional or inter-site cost comparisons. However, if this is considered
an objective of the exercise, the difficulties relating to comparisons
mentioned earlier in the book should be kept in mind.

Specifying the elements and categories against which to apportion
time can lead to inaccuracies if not thought out carefully. If the individual concerned does not think that the elements are appropriate to
their work they will not bother to make accurate entries. It may be as
well therefore, in the early stages, to get participants to specify their
own element definitions, or cooperate to provide a comprehensive listing at the outset of the exercise.

In making the above comments it is presupposed that the intention
is to build up a reasonably accurate and detailed picture of how and
where quality-related costs are incurred. However, as mentioned earlier
in this chapter, not all quality management practitioners accept that
this is necessary. An alternative view is that it is necessary only to
identify and analyse the high-cost areas with a view to mounting specific cost-cutting projects. Yet another view is that periodic snapshots of
the quality-related cost situation (as opposed to continuous monitoring)
are all that is needed. The incidence of such diverse objectives with
their differing requirements serves to reinforce the case for a rational
approach in which the purposes of the exercise are clearly established
at the outset.

Against the background of difficulties with definitions of knowing what should be included amongst quality-related costs, and the problems of gathering some of the costs, there seems little point in pursuing accuracy even where it is known to be obtainable. On the other hand, costs must be accurate enough to be credible even to those whose efficiency or performance is perhaps impugned by the resulting report. Nevertheless, many companies are content with quality costings which are accurate to ±10% and, seemingly, the greater the cost, the greater the tolerance. A cost report which does not have credibility is a waste of time and, unfortunately, the credibility of a whole report can easily be seriously undermined by a skilled protagonist once a single weakness has been exposed. It is for this reason that only costs produced or endorsed by accounts departments should be used in the report. Costs produced by accounts department have greater acceptability and are more likely to be compatible and consistent with other cost efficiency measures.

A final point on the matter of accuracy is that guesses are at best useless. As already mentioned, experience has shown that where people are involved in disparate activities estimates by personnel, their colleagues and supervisors tend to be long-term based and vary widely. The danger of course is that the guesses are either ascribed the same credence as other figures in the report, or they may be identified as a weakness through which the report may be discredited. They will certainly not be kept in their proper perspective.

3.7 The people involved in quality cost collection

In some companies, accountants give the impression that they consider quality assurance as a necessary evil, and consequently there are attempts to play down the true costs or savings from quality improvement activities. On the other hand, engineers and technical and quality assurance specialists are also culpable in making simple operations appear to accountants to be very technical, difficult and complicated. These are important factors which tend to inhibit the collection and use of quality cost data in some companies. Everyone who has tried to investigate costs will almost certainly have experienced the frustration caused by the communication barrier which separates the professional accountant from the non-accountant.

An essential precursor to collecting quality-related costs is knowledge of the company in terms of history, culture, people, processes and products. This is not as might at first be imagined an unnecessary consideration for a company carrying out a quality cost exercise. A quality costing exercise requires quality, technical, and accounting knowledge, and few people at the right level in the organization are likely to have all the knowledge which is necessary.

Thus costing should be a joint exercise. If accounts people try to do it alone, they are likely to miss a lot of the detail or even be misled by people with axes to grind. The accountants usually seek guidance from quality assurance staff on what to measure. On the other hand, if quality assurance and technical people go it alone they may, for example, fail to discover costs which tidy-minded accountants have tucked away out of sight, and consequently the costs collected and presented will lack credibility. In addition they may not be aware of the true meaning or relative sensitivity of certain cost data. It should be remembered, however, that management accountants are always under pressure to produce all sorts of costs and, if quality costing is to get off the ground in a company, they need to be convinced that there is some worth in the exercise.

3.8 The views of quality managers and accountants

An interesting feature of the treatment of measurement and collection of cost data is the contrast between the apparent optimism of the majority of quality management specialists about how easy it should be (at least to get started) and the caution of the accountants and a few quality management specialists. This interdisciplinary difference of outlook is so marked that those from the quality fraternity who advocate caution are made to appear as spiritless pessimists who are more aware of the obstacles than of the opportunities. However, deeper study reveals that despite their apparent optimism about the ease of measurement of costs, most quality management specialists acknowledge that it may take years to establish a good system of measurement and collection. Reasons for the differences in outlook may arise from fundamentally different perceptions of costing exercises. It is clear that most quality management specialists think in terms of pilot schemes or improvement projects requiring approximate costs to be measured in a small segment of the business. Accountants on the other hand are professionally, if not naturally, concerned with the precision and completeness of costs. They therefore wish to see how the mini-exercise or improvement project stands in relation to the whole business. This of course requires much more information to be got out, much of which may appear to the quality assurance professional to be irrelevant.

The differences have also given rise to (or at least reinforced) prejudices amongst the quality fraternity about accountants and accounting systems. Whilst there are indeed difficulties, it is being less than fair to the current breed of management accountants to suggest that they cannot or will not accommodate the needs of quality assurance and technical specialists requiring data which are out of the ordinary.

3.9 Commitment of senior management

As a final point it is important to remember that, in addition to having the necessary mechanism in place for collecting quality-related costs, it is also necessary for the Chief Executive Officer and members of the senior management team to have the will and commitment to support the quality cost collection process and the use of the data.

References

1. Leibert, F. P. (1968) Guidelines on the gathering and implementation of quality costs. *Qual. Eng.*, **32**, (2), 39–43.
2. Jenney, B. W. (1974) Motivation for quality. *Qual. Eng.*, **38**, (1), 5–7.
3. Juran, J. M. and Gryna, F. (1980) *Quality Planning and Analysis*, McGraw-Hill, New York.
4. Juran, J. M. (ed.) (1988) *Quality Control Handbook*, McGraw-Hill, New York.
5. Payne, B. J. (1990) The quality improvement process in service areas, in *Managing Quality* (ed. B. G. Dale and J. J. Plunkett), Philip Allan, Hemel Hempstead, Hertfordshire, ch. 20.
6. Feigenbaum, A. V. (1983) *Total Quality Control*, McGraw-Hill, New York.
7. Hallum, S. and Casperson, R. (1975) Economy and quality control. *Proc. 19th EOQC Conf., Venice*, pp. 11–22.
8. Blank, L. and Solorzano, J. (1978) Using quality cost analysis for management improvement. *Ind. Eng.*, **10**, (2), 46–51.
9. Booth, W. E. (1976) Financial reporting of quality performance. *Qual. Prog.*, 14–15.
10. Alford, R. E. (1979) Quality costs – where to start – Part I. *Quality*, 36–7.
11. Alford, R. E. (1979) Quality costs – where to start – Part II. *Quality*, 70–1.
12. Alford, R. E. (1979) Quality costs – where to start – Part III. *Quality*, 40–2.
13. BS 6143: Part 2 (1990) *Guide to the Economics of Quality – Prevention, Appraisal and Failure Model*, British Standards Institution, London.
14. ASQC Quality Costs Committee (1974) *Quality Costs: What and How*, American Society for Quality Control, Milwaukee, WI.
15. Ross, O. T., *et al.* (1980) *Architects Manual ICAM Definition Method, IDEFO*, CAM-i Inc., Texas.

16. Marsh, J. (1989) Process modelling for quality improvement, *Proc. Second Int. Conf. on Total Quality Management, London*, IFS Publications, Bedford, pp. 111–21.

17. BS 6143: Part 1 (1991) *Guide to the Economics of Quality – Process Cost Model*, British Standards Institution, London.

18. Crossfield, R. T. (1989) A study of some key techniques used in planning for total quality management, *MSc Thesis*, Manchester School of Management, UMIST.

19. Crossfield, R. T. and Dale, B. G. (1990) Mapping quality assurance systems: a methodology. *Qual. Reliab. Eng. Int.*, **6**, (3), 167–78.

4
Reporting of quality costs

4.1 Introduction

The objectives of quality cost collection and the views on what costs should or should not be collected on a regular basis have been discussed in Chapter 3. This chapter examines the key issues to be considered in the reporting of quality costs.

The growth of interest in product and service quality as a key contributor to competitiveness and marketability has stimulated organizational concern for the economic effects of quality. Companies are now beginning to amass and use quality cost data but in a limited way, using mainly scrap and rework analysis and warranty claims. It is encouraging to find such facts being used even if they are not assembled as a formalized quality costing report. Because scrap and rework costs frequently amount to an impressive sum of money, there is often a tendency to assume it is the whole cost, or indeed a reluctance to investigate more closely in case it turns out to be even larger.

It should be noted that the reporting of quality costs is only touched upon by writers on the subject of quality costing.

4.2 Extracting quality costs from existing company systems

Quality cost information needs to be produced from a company's existing system; it is easier to develop a quality costing system in a 'greenfield's' situation as opposed to attempting to break into an established system. A common fallacy is that larger companies have accounting systems from which it is relatively easy to extract quality-related costs. In general, such companies have large immutable accounting systems and practices which are often imposed by a head office function with little flexibility to provide quality costs; the situation is compounded if the head office is located in another country. On the other hand, smaller companies are less likely to have a full-time professionally qualified person responsible for management accounting.

Some of the difficulties in obtaining quality cost data are related to organizational structures and with the accountancy systems used. Few companies set up matrix accounting systems which allow costs to be collected by topic (e.g. product and service quality) across the traditional functional groups (e.g. sales, production/operations, research and development) and it is seldom the case that all the costs attributable to a topic such as quality are incurred under a single cost centre. There is a widely held view that cost information is easily obtainable if a company wishes to obtain it. The authors do not agree with this view. For example, Eldridge and Dale [1] reporting on a quality costing exercise carried out in an organization employing around 200 personnel and manufacturing industrial valves state:

> Very little information existed in a form that could be directly transferred into a quality cost report. Much of the quality cost information was buried so deep in the accounting system that retrieval was impracticable. On the other hand, a considerable amount of information lay dormant.

Companies which collect quality costs have developed their systems as one aspect of gathering quality-related information in attempting to monitor quality performance. Another factor has been the economic and competitive pressure which has caused companies to look in more detail at appraisal activities and the costs of failure, with a view to facilitating improvements and reducing costs. Such companies have based their systems and methods on what they are doing in terms of the technology, product type, processes, dealings with suppliers and customers, etc., rather than on any published list of cost elements, or categorization into the classical activities of prevention, appraisal and failure. The systems which have been developed are usually concerned only with inspection, failure and rework.

4.3 Some fundamentals of quality cost reporting

In order for matters to become part of a routine costing system it is first necessary to record the activity or transaction routinely. Once it has been decided which costs are relevant to the organization, and which are insignificant, it is important to collect and display all those costs which have been decided upon, and also to indicate the existence, by a suitable description, of the relevant costs which cannot yet be quantified. This is important because, firstly, reporting only part of the costs, without some form of qualification, can be very misleading, and, secondly, reporting the existence of unquantified costs keeps them in view of management and encourages attempts to find ways of measuring them.

The creation of a quality-related cost file, integrated with existing costing systems but perhaps with some additional expense codes, should not present many problems – collecting the data will be much more difficult. Those quality cost elements which come from within the quality assurance department may be easy to obtain but those from other departments may be more difficult, especially if it is suspected that the data may be used to attack them and their staff in some future improvement activity. Nevertheless, provision should be made in the file for collecting such data, even though it may take a long time to obtain satisfactory returns on a routine basis.

A popular view amongst quality management practitioners is that quality cost reports should indicate the origin of failure costs by department (e.g. design, production, engineering, purchasing, marketing, etc.), in the hope that adverse publicity will provoke remedial action. Unfortunately, it may also antagonize departmental managers so that they become uncooperative in providing information for the report. It may even result in the deliberate obscuring of quality performance evidence and other counter-productive actions. Proclaiming the sins of others is not guaranteed to win cooperation. Emphasis on improvement opportunities rather than attribution of failures may help to avoid such difficulties. It should also not be forgotten that having an effective internal customer/supplier relationship in place is a key feature of an organization's TQM efforts.

It should go without saying that the purpose of a quality-related cost report is not primarily to promote the interests of the quality assurance department. Neither is it to display the quality cost contributions of other departments; such analyses are secondary objectives and should only be stated in the context of actual and achievable performance and the known real constraints as, for example, in a project format.

In the companies studied by the authors, reporting on quality costs was found, in the main, to be a subsection of the general reporting of the quality assurance department's activities, and as such loses its impact. For maximum impact quality costs should be included in a company's overall cost reporting system. It could even be considered as the subject of a separate management report. Unfortunately, the lack of sophistication of quality cost collection and measurement is such that it does not allow quality cost reporting to be carried out in the same detail and to the same standard as, for example, the production/operation and marketing functions.

Senior managers are like everyone else in wanting easy decisions to make. Having costs, which are the bases of business decisions, tangled up with technical and quality information make the data less clear than they could be and often provide an excuse to defer a decision. The problem for senior managers should not be to disentangle and analyse data in order to decide what to do: it should be to decide whether to act, choose which course of action to pursue, ensure provision of necessary resources, and by comparing the quality costs with those budgeted assess the effectiveness of the planned improvements. Problems, possible solutions and their resource requirements should be presented in the context of accountability centres which have the necessary authority, if not the resources, to execute the decisions of the senior management team.

Overall the standard of reporting of quality costs encountered in the course of the authors' research is poor. Good standards are essential if reports are to make an impact and provoke action.

However, it should be noted that putting costs on quality-related matters and reporting them is only a first step towards drawing the issue of product and service quality more into the business arena.

4.4 Reporting formats

As might be expected, organizations use a variety of quality cost reporting formats and methods of presenting the data.

Presentation of costs under prevention, appraisal, and internal and external failure is the most popular approach for reporting quality costs, albeit with different cost elements appropriate to different industries as discussed in Chapter 3. This format is favoured by quality assurance managers perhaps because, on the face of it, it forms a balance sheet for the quality function with prevention equivalent to investment, appraisal to operating cost, and failure to (negative) profit. However, in some industries the time lags arising between action and effect are such that concurrent expenditures on, say, prevention activities and external failure such as warranty claims, bear no relation whatever to each other.

An important consideration in the presentation of quality-related costs are the needs of the recipients and it may be worth presenting information in several different formats according to particular interests and likely use of the information. For example, weekly reports of costs and scrap and rework are of greatest value to shopfloor supervisors, and monthly reports of total costs, highlighting current problems and progress with quality improvement projects, would be most suitable for middle management, while total costs and costs to act on are needed by the Chief Executive Officer and members of the senior management team. While selective reporting of this type has its merits, it should be done against a background of the total cost of quality.

Consideration should also be given to displaying quality cost data as part of an organization's visual management system; Pareto diagrams are a good method for presenting such data. In this way information is diffused rapidly and is a valuable method of encouraging everyone in the organization to assist in reducing the costs of non-conformance.

Some organizations employ a two-tier quality costing reporting system. Each department identifies the major costs of non-conformance which are specific to them and the departmental manager is responsible for activating improvement projects to reduce these costs. The key non-conformance costs on a company-wide basis are identified and individual executives made responsible for their reduction. The reporting of both departmental and company key quality costs are carried out on a monthly basis.

A point worthy of note is that the time lag between manufacture, the sale of the product, and warranty claim and payment is often so long that warranty costs should not be reported in the same context as current quality costs. In some cases the warranty and guarantee period may not be initiated until several years after the sale of the product to the customer. Such a time lag can considerably distort the quality performance of the organization as depicted by the level of quality-related costs. If the effects of the time lag and the effects of price changes, inflation, exchange rates, etc. are added, there can be no doubt that warranty costs ought to be reported as a separate category of quality cost and not considered in the context of current quality costs. In the context of other (non-quality) costs they should be reported as a loss, and related to other losses (and profits).

4.5 'Economic cost of equality' models

It is apparent that the costs and economics of many quality-related activities, including investment in prevention and appraisal activities, are not known. It is perhaps surprising therefore to find in the literature a number of diagrammatic representations of quality cost models which purport to show relationships between the major quality cost categories. Many discussions of quality costs in the literature feature such a model, but many quality management practitioners are doubtful about the representations and feel that they can be misleading.

The general suppositions underlying all these notional models are that investment in prevention and appraisal activities will bring handsome rewards from reduced failure costs, and that further investment in prevention activities will show profits from reduced appraisal costs.

However, despite these common principles there are wide differences between some of the models.

Plunkett and Dale [2] have examined in detailed these various notional models and the main findings of this piece of research are summarized below.

• There is a striking dissimilarity between the notional models (e.g. Besterfield [3], Harrington [4] and Juran [5]) and those based on actual data (e.g. Campanella and Corcoran [6], Huckett [7] and Hagan [8]).

• The notional models conveniently and, in some cases, inexplicably combine major quality cost categories. The combination of cost categories is dependent upon the objective of the quality costing exercise. If, for example, the objective is to reduce failure costs, there may be little point in distinguishing between prevention and appraisal costs. If, on the other hand, the objective is to reduce failure and/or appraisal costs, then perhaps it is not important to separate them. It is worth noting that the notional models do not distinguish between internal and external failure costs; some models combine prevention and appraisal costs, thereby suggesting that reduction of failure costs by increasing the combined expenditure on prevention and appraisal is the prime strategy for reducing quality costs. In fact, reduction of appraisal costs by increasing preventive measures may be a reasonable and worthwhile alternative.

• There are a diversity of measures of quality used as the abscissae in indicating the relationship between the major quality cost categories. The models based on real data are plotted against a linear time base rather than against some measure of quality performance.

• Some of the models imply nonsensically extravagant returns on investment in prevention and/or appraisal. Indeed, it is noticeable that whenever investment in prevention expenditure is discussed there is an implicit expectation of a large return on the investment. Investments in prevention through capital or resources often involve stepwise increases because of the generally low level of expenditure on prevention, but are never represented as such by the models. While recognizing that companies are in business to make profit, and that there may be competition for limited resources, the paybacks expected (and sometimes proffered) from investment in quality improvement activities seem unusually high, and since high returns are usually associated with high risk, one wonders whether, as a general rule, the benefits from investment in prevention are seen in business circles as being problematical.

• There is little hard evidence to support the notion that quality cost curves are exponential and give rise to cost minima.

The view that many of the widely publicized quality economics models are inaccurate, and may even be of the wrong form, is widely supported by quality assurance managers. Everyone would like to have a valid model which they could use to assess their present situation and predict the effects of changes. So far as is known there are insufficient data available to construct such a model, though there should be enough collective experience available to make a reasonable hypothesis as to the shape and the relative proportions of the constituent costs in the diagram. For example, there are reasonably good grounds for believing that optimum quality, if it exists, is near to the highest attainable standard of quality. The model should take account of the fact that investments in prevention through capital or resources often involve relatively large stepwise increases. It should also reflect the often considerable time lag to be expected between investment in prevention and/or appraisal and reduction in failure costs, and especially warranty costs.

References

1. Eldridge, S. and Dale, B. G. (1989) Quality costing: the lessons learnt from a study carried out in two phases. *Eng. Costs Prod. Econ.*, **18**, (1), 33–44.
2. Plunkett, J. J. and Dale, B. G. (1988) Quality costs: a critique of some 'Economic cost of quality' models. *Int. J. Prod. Res.*, **26**, (11), 1713–26.
3. Besterfield, D. H. (1979) *Quality Control*, Prentice-Hall, Englewood Cliffs, NJ.
4. Harrington, J. H. (1976) Quality costs – the whole and its parts – Part 1. *Quality*, **15**, (5), 34–5.
5. Juran, J. M. (ed.) (1988) *Quality Control Handbook*, McGraw-Hill, New York.
6. Campanella, J. and Corcoran, F. J. (1983) Principles of quality costs. *Qual. Prog.*, **16**, (4), 16–21.
7. Huckett, J. D. (1985) An outline of the quality improvement process. *Int. J. Qual. Reliab. Manage.*, **2**, (2), 5–14.
8. Hagan, J. T. (1986) Quality costs, in *Quality Management Handbook* (eds. L. Walsh, R. Wurster and R. J. Kimber), Marcel Dekker, ch. 7. New York.

5
Uses of quality costs

5.1 Categories of uses

The majority of authors on the subject of quality costing focus on the use of quality costs. Indeed there is no point in collecting cost information if it is not to be used. Its usefulness is the only justification for its collection and clearly this is one of the most important criteria in setting up a cost collection system. Most organizations are looking to quality cost data to show things that their other quality-related data do not reveal. This requirement raises two interesting points. Firstly, in requiring cost data to be more useful than other data, it is implicit that use or usefulness is the principal criterion in collecting data. Secondly, it may not be necessary for cost data actually to add anything to other data on which they are based. Their usefulness may lie solely in being expressed in monetary terms. In our experience companies tend to identify situations they would like to achieve through the use of cost information. By and large, questions about uses do not elicit answers which are specifically cost oriented (e.g. set cost-reduction targets and establish cost efficiency measures).

It should be noted that the lack of routine quality costing information does not hinder an organization from pursuing quality improvement projects which have been identified from technical and/or quality assurance data. It is, however, a handicap in setting overall cost-reduction targets.

The uses of quality costs are numerous and diverse. However, they may be grouped into three broad categories. Firstly, quality costs may be used to promote product and service quality as a business parameter; secondly, they give rise to performance measures and facilitate improvement activities; and, thirdly, they provide the means for planning and controlling future quality costs.

5.2 Promoting quality as a business parameter

This first use – promoting quality as a business parameter – is usually expressed as attracting the attention of the board of directors and the senior management team by using their language (i.e. money) in order to help shock them into action in relation to quality improvement. However, Eldridge and Dale [1] warn that if the costs collected are substantially less than the typical 10–20% figure of annual sales turnover, which by now most managers are familiar with, it could work in the opposite manner and help to convince senior managers that the quality performance of the organization is satisfactory when it is not. It should also be pointed out that any first attempts to collect quality-related costs are likely to underestimate them. Additional cost elements tend to be identified as organizational quality costing expertise is developed. A number of managers have pointed out to the authors that when their organization's quality costs do not match up to this 10–20% figure there is a tendency to believe that key costs have made promoting a drive to look for the 'missing' costs.

There is little doubt that costs help to keep quality aspects of the business in the spotlight – but only if featured in the regular management accounts and reporting system. In promoting quality as an important business parameter some people go even further by using costs to illustrate that it is not only the quality assurance department who are involved in quality but also everyone's work impinges on the quality of the product and/or service, and to promote ownership for quality improvement. The success of gatherers and presenters of quality-related costs in promoting quality by means of costs is difficult to gauge. So far as is known there has been no formal study to determine how Chief Executive Officers who are aware of the importance of quality became so. It is clear from the authors' research that many executives got the message without having quality cost information to hand. Indeed in some cases it is the other way around, in that a belief in the importance of product and service quality to corporate health has prompted a quality cost investigation.

We have encountered the situation where the nature of the technology and processes is such that scrap accounts for one-quarter of a company's total costs. Some organizations, having once identified their major quality costs, become very concerned about the magnitude of the cost of scrap and rework. They often have no reason to suppose that their competitors are significantly less efficient than they are themselves, and recognize that such high scrap costs could make them uncompetitive if their competitors achieve substantial breakthroughs in their technology process management and subsequently improve their yields. This must surely engender very different behaviour and attitudes to product and service quality than in those organizations where the situation is not so severe. The same is true in the case of organizations who have to scrap all non-conforming products. There is little doubt that high direct expenditures on quality-related matters seem to be acceptable to companies whose quality standards are necessarily very high and determined by mandatory regulation. For companies in these types of situations, product and service quality is not just about saving cost and improving profitability: it must be fundamental to all their business vision, mission, and activities. Hence, for them, quality costing should be akin to business accounting.

Knowledge of quality-related costs enables business decisions about quality to be made in an objective manner. It permits the use of sensitivity analyses, discounted cash flow and other accounting methods and techniques for the evaluation of expenditure projects as in any other area of the business. In this way it helps companies to decide how, when and where to invest in prevention activities or equipment. This is a most valuable use of cost data. But even if full cost data were available they may not be useful for this purpose, because in many organizations the fundamental economics of prevention and/or appraisal do not seem to be well understood. Indeed, it is noticeable that whenever investment in prevention expenditure is discussed there is an implicit expectation of a large return on the investment. Progressive companies are always looking for profitable ways to invest in quality improvement activities, but their task is made very difficult by the lack of data and understanding of the economics of investment in quality improvement activities.

Scrap, rectification and rework costs are collected and reported in most companies and are regarded as important costs which feature in companies' business decisions. Most companies would confidently claim that the decision whether or not to do corrective work or to scrap a product or batch is taken on economic grounds. Not so. Our research indicates that the economics of scrapping or rectification are by no means clear in many companies. A major difficulty encountered in this is the valuation to be placed on scrapped goods. Some popular views encountered are that the value should be the selling price, the market price, the raw materials price or the materials cost plus the cost of processing to the point of scrapping. These different bases will obviously give rise to very different valuations, which may not matter if the costs are not to be used in deciding courses of action. However, most companies claim that the decision whether to scrap or rectify is taken on economic grounds; so if the real cost is not known, how can sensible economic decisions be made? To complicate matters further, the decision about whether to scrap or rework is often taken by personnel who do not have access to the financial information necessary to make an economic choice. And in any case the economics will vary depending on workload, customer pressure, contractual requirements, urgency of delivery, etc. In many organizations the scrap versus rework decisions are based primarily on ease of rework, available capacity and production output, and delivery targets rather than on cost. One may pose the question that if the true economics of rework are known why is there so much difficulty in putting a value on scrap? In the light of this scrap versus rework decisions are more influenced by engineering knowledge, production need, overtime policies, etc. against a background of a general feel for costs, than by the true economics of the situation.

Continuing on this theme it should also be noted that recouping scrap and costs from suppliers is not as efficiently done as might be expected, even though it is written into the purchasing agreement. Most companies are successful only in recovering materials costs. Rectification costs incurred owing to supplier faults are not usually recovered. An anomaly uncovered at one company studied was that management claimed to agree possible sorting and rework charges with suppliers before starting work on the raw materials, but did not know their own in-house economics of scrap and rework. Perhaps there are *ad hoc* methods of estimating costs to be charged back to the suppliers which are unsuited to estimating in-house costs because they would be incompatible with other in-house methods and costs.

Despite this, there are many opportunities for investment in prevention, with consequential real cost savings. Employing qualified experienced staff, encouraging study, facilitating the education of all employees, and providing training are examples of investment in personnel. Investment in supplier quality assurance and assistance through supplier development, assessment, auditing and rating, and joint improvement activities through teamwork are claimed by many companies to pay handsome dividends. Of direct interest to production engineers and technical specialists are the possibilities of effecting savings through investment in tooling, processes and equipment. Nonconforming tooling is frequently responsible for excess work and the extra costs of improved production tooling is often a worthwhile investment. At one company studied, the quality assurance manager noted that operator gauging time was interfering with the machining operation. Investment in electronic gauging equipment was comfortably justified on grounds of increased productivity. The extra data available from the equipment have also been of value in assessing, controlling and improving machine and process capability.

It is often found that a knowledge of quality costs is of considerable benefit in the education of staff in the concept of TQM as a key business parameter and gaining their commitment to a process of continuous quality improvement. The level of quality costs is often fed back to staff in the form of diagnostic reports and surveys and this opens up dialogue on what are the major areas for improvement. This knowledge of quality costs helps to justify and reinforce the need for TQM and reduces scepticism as to why the organization is setting out on the TQM journey.

Looking forward, aspects of quality that will need to be developed if the business aspects of quality are to be raised from the level of *ad hoc* cost reports and occasional cost-reduction exercises to the level enjoyed by other major business parameters are as follows.

1. Quality cost performance indicators. Quality assurance managers are keen to use cost data to monitor internal quality performance in cost-sensitive areas, and to establish bases against which to gauge overall quality cost performance.
2. Investment criteria. While it may be axiomatic that prevention is better than cure, it is often difficult to justify investment in prevention activities. To some extent such investments are regarded as blind acts of faith. Little is known and nothing has been published on the appropriate levels and timing of investments, payoffs or payback periods.

    The relatively low level of expenditure on prevention activities (cf. appraisal and failure) is stressed by every quality cost analyst. The majority of managers would like to deploy a greater proportion of quality-related expenditures on prevention but have no data to support their arguments. It is even doubtful whether the true economics of investment in appraisal versus failure costs are known in many companies.
3. Quality efficiency indices. Business efficiencies are commonly analysed and expressed using a variety of criteria (most financial). Maintenance and improvement of quality are not among the criteria used. Quality assurance manager's efforts to persuade fellow managers and directors of the value of product and service quality to an organization's corporate health are often frustrated by a lack of well-known and accepted indices or standards. Some companies have developed measures for the purpose of internally monitoring quality improvement but no general guidelines or methods of calculation exist which would readily allow a company to assess its standards against a norm or other companies.
4. Specific problems of quality costing requiring attention are:
    (a) costs of equipment downtime;

(b)   the economics of machine and process capability versus higher capital cost of equipment;

(c)   extra costs incurred due to order-splitting;

(d)   costs arising from concessions, modifications, design/engineering and document changes.

5.3 Facilitating performance measures and improvement activities

The second use – giving rise to performance measures – is a most popular one. Whilst there are a wide variety of specific uses they can be conveniently categorized under a few headings. Costs may be expressed as absolute costs (including costs per unit of output or sales turnover) or as relative costs (i.e. as indices or ratios to other business costs). These cost measures are used for three main purposes: (1) comparison with other parts of the business or with other businesses, (2) decision-making, and (3) motivation.

There are serious limitations which constrain the usefulness of absolute cost data as already described in this book. Indices and ratios are used to facilitate comparison. The coverage of indices and ratios in the quality costing literature, apart from some general advice on making sure that the factors used to derive the index are in fact related to each other, and that single ratios often do not tell the whole story and may always need to be considered alongside other ratios, is disappointing and lacks conviction. Perhaps indices are too specific to particular situations to make general writing on the subject easy or worthwhile, or perhaps they are just not very telling. The expression of quality costs as a percentage of the works' recovered costs is a particularly good example of a ratio because the level of overhead is always under the organizational spotlight. Relating quality costs to other costs which are well known and are always under scrutiny for reduction may cause quality costs to become so too. When quality costs are presented in such a way that they are seen as a way for increasing profitability, executives' attention automatically becomes focused on them.

Despite the many warnings against making comparisons, there is no escaping the desire for data for comparison purposes to assess performance. Companies are keen to know if their quality performance in terms of quality-related costs is good, bad or indifferent. However, it is dangerous to compare quality cost data between different companies, industries and service situations unless the accounting practices used and how the costs were computed are known and comparable. At present, every company's method of calculation is probably unique to that company. Internal comparisons are fine, but it is external comparisons which should be treated with caution. Comparisons between sets of quality cost data from different sources should be discouraged and restricted to examining costs before and after specific quality improvement projects and activities have been completed, and improvement with time (though this also can have many pitfalls).

Some would say there is a need for published data so that companies which collect quality costs have a yardstick against which to judge their performance. The most popular comparative measures are sales, manufacturing costs, unadjusted value-added against quality costs. Whilst quality costs are useful, they need to be supplemented with other, non-cost, data when making specific decisions. It should not be forgotten that important differences between individual company's costs is reflected not by how much is spent, but by how it is spent.

Confidentiality of cost information is often the greatest barrier to its publication and accountants are much more reluctant to reveal cost information than their quality assurance, engineering or technical counterparts. The authors have noticed, in their research into TQM, that on a number of occasions company personnel, who clearly were being very frank in their answers to questions, became hesitant and uncertain when it came to discussing costs. Contacting accountants to seek clarification on data did not help. Indeed, in some cases it seemed to have the opposite effect to that intended and respondents became even more reticent, almost as if they had been 'warned off'. The case for confidentiality of some costs is questionable on a number of counts. Firstly, published costs need not be current data. Secondly, quality costs are perhaps only 10–20% of selling price. Thirdly, the nature of quality costs is such that no indication of a company's most important or sensitive costs is likely to be gleaned from analysis of them. Management accountants could do their profession and quality assurance managers a service by examining just how confidential quality costs need to be instead of labelling them 'confidential', perhaps because they have not taken the trouble to think about them. Making cost information more freely available would provide considerable assistance to those managers trying to get their board of directors to invest in a process of quality improvement; it could also be used within the company for motivational purposes. Fourthly, for many standard products a competent production engineer/technical specialist could probably construct a fairly accurate manufacturing cost profile anyway, and, fifthly, confidential costs could readily be disguised by multiplying them by an arbitrary factor.

Perhaps confidentiality was the problem when Sullivan and Owens [2] tried to collect quality cost information from an ASQC survey. Perhaps many fewer companies collect costs than would be expected. (Surveys in the UK and Ireland suggest about one-third of companies collect quality-related costs of any kind.) Perhaps ASQC members were not interested enough to respond. Whatever the reason, the response rate of approximately 0.1% to 35 000 enquiries does not provide grounds for optimism that costs for comparison purposes are likely to be freely available in the near future.

The cross-industry surveys of Gilmore [3] and the journal *Quality* [4] contain limited amounts of data which are interesting. Both sets of data show clearly that there are large industry-to-industry variations. Although the editor of *Quality* specifically warns against making comparisons there are strong grounds for suspecting from their data that companies which have a more sophisticated system of quality costing appear to have a better quality performance (or is it vice versa?). Gilmore [3, 5] attempts to extract more out of his data than is really warranted and is relatively rash compared with other authors on the subject of quality costing in his assertions concerning the comparability of his data.

To be of real value data should be accurate and complete. Lack of qualification of much of the published data makes it difficult to take anything but a circumspect view of them. Many figures are so similar (especially the division of costs between prevention, appraisal and failure) that one wonders whether they all originated from the same source. Similarities in the distribution of costs within industry categories also prompt the thought that there may, possibly, be quality cost structures which are characteristic of particular industries (i.e. in the same way that different industries have characteristic materials, wage and overhead cost ratios).

Use of quality costs for decision-making is mostly restricted to choices between competing cost-reduction or quality improvement projects and management time and resources, initiating corrective action and setting targets for cost reductions. In a study of quality-related decision-making, Duncalf and Dale [6] found no evidence of other uses and this is corroborated by the present authors' research findings. Uses for motivational purposes include display to shopfloor workers of scrap costs arising within their department, and to emphasize to middle managers their departments' contribution to total quality costs. Both are examples of the principle of accountability and ownership being used.

Quality costs are also used to identify products, processes and departments for investigation, to set cost-reduction targets, and to measure progress towards targets. It is worth pointing out that the authors' research has also revealed that ranking of competing improvement projects by different cost bases and by numbers gave very different indicators. The preferred base depends on factors and circumstances that may change with time or with a company's business situation. Different indicators may require very different amounts and types of resources. They may be used to evaluate the cost benefit of individual quality-related activities (e.g. quality system certification, FMEA, design of experiments, SPC, and supplier development). Quality costs are clearly a useful tool for initiating improvement projects and levers for uncovering quality problems. Quality improvement projects appear to offer the quickest route to useful exploitation of cost data. Utilization of total quality costs takes much longer.

Another possible use of costs in the broad category of improvement activities is that quality costing might focus attention on the chronic problems for which compensations had been built into the system. The argument (which is an integral part of Juran's [7] teaching) goes that sporadic problems can be, and are, readily picked up by other means (e.g. statistical process control) but that the results of chronic problems are built into the base values, against which judgements are made. Obvious examples are allowances for material loss and average scrap levels built into standard costs, but there must be many other examples (e.g. personnel and equipment on standby, additional supervision, extra stocks, etc.). To expose all such costs and reduce and eliminate wastage would require a very wide view of TQM along the lines of world-class companies, and a ruthless and relentless pursuit of truth and continuous and never-ending improvement to be adopted.

5.4 Planning and control

The use of quality costs as a means of planning and controlling quality costs is widely mooted in the literature. Costs are the bases for budgeting and eventual cost control. Many writers on the subject of quality costing list budgetary control as the ultimate objective. Despite this, there is a lack of convincing arguments or examples to support the objective. In general, the use of budgetary control of quality-related costs, though popular in concept, is not well examined in the literature.

Contributions from the quality assurance fraternity tend to see establishment of quality cost budgets for the purpose of controlling cost as the ultimate goal which may be achieved after accumulating a lot of data over a long time in pursuit of quality improvements for specific cost reductions. Morse [8], on the other hand, sees the prime purpose of a quality cost system as being to give management a means of planning and controlling quality costs. Other accountants seem to go along with this view but Cox [9] qualifies it when he points out that there are instances where product and service quality cannot be a matter for compromise and that only in those situations where the only result of failure is a loss of profit can trade-offs be made. Balancing Cox's [9] circumspection is Claret's [10] optimism about the level of sophistication that may be achieved in planning and controlling quality costs. Unfortunately no one shares his optimism or, if they do, they are reluctant to say so in print.

Whilst the theme of planning and control is popular with writers, there are surprisingly few examples in the literature of its application to quality costs. With the exception of Burns [11] who describes the use of costs to predict warranty expenditures it seems to be assumed that conventional expenditure control is the main purpose. An example uncovered by the authors from their research was the use of quality costs to provide information on future quotations for products or contracts having onerous quality and manufacturing conditions.

In terms of planning and control again it must be stressed that the fundamental economics of appraisal are not known in most companies. High costs of failure are apparently used to justify inspection and its frequency, without any attempts being made to determine the true economic balance. It is somewhat surprising that the economics of inspection are not well established and widely known in view of the fact that inspection-oriented approaches to quality control have predominated in manufacturing industry for many decades. There is evidence of the potential for cost reductions by drastic reductions in inspection forces apparently without loss of quality. It is expected that there would be little change in first-off inspection unless the capability of machines and tools to sustain tolerances was improved, but that the patrol and final inspection activity could be reduced through the effective use of SPC.

It should be noted that in organizations manufacturing products on a 'one-off' basis with long manufacturing lead times there is little opportunity to build up a historical file of meaningful cost data for use in planning and control. Companies in these kinds of situations are often restricted to the use of costs in the context of improvement projects.

References

1. Eldridge, S. and Dale, B. G. (1989) Quality costings: the lessons learnt from a study carried out in two phases. *Eng. Costs Prod. Econ.*, **18**, (1), 33–44.
2. Sullivan, E., and Owens, D. A. (1983) Catching a glimpse of quality costs today. *Qual. Prog.*, 21–4.
3. Gilmore, H. L. (1983) Consumer product quality control cost revisited. *Qual. Prog.* 28–32.
4. Anon (1977) Quality cost survey. *Quality*, 20–2.
5. Gilmore, H. L. (1984) Consumer product quality costs, *Proc. World Quality Congr., Brighton*, pp. 587–95.
6. Duncalf, A. J. and Dale, B. G. (1985) How British industry is

making decisions on product quality. *Long Range Plann*. **18**, (5), 81–8.

7. Juran, J. M. (1988) *Quality Control Handbook*, McGraw-Hill, New York.
8. Morse, W. J. (1983) Measuring quality costs. *Cost Manage.*, **July/ August**, 16–20.
9. Cox, B. (1982) The role of the management accountant in quality costing. *Qual. Assur.*, **8**, (3), 82–4.
10. Claret, J. (1981) Never mind the quality? *Manage. Acc.*, 24–6.
11. Burns, V. P. (1970) Warranty prediction: putting a $ on poor quality. *Qual. Prog.*, 28–9.

6
Case study, company 1

6.1 Introduction

Company 1 is a member of a large group of companies engaged in metal refining and fabrication of a very diverse range of metal products. It is a fully integrated manufacturing unit making products from refined and prepared raw materials. The headquarters of the division in which the company is located are sited at a sister factory some 40 miles away. The company's products are supplied to vehicle and traction equipment manufacturers via a holding and warehousing operation which also supplies a network of agencies and service centres with spares and replacement products.

At the factory where the quality costing investigation was carried out the company manufactures heat exchange ancillaries for automotive and traction equipment. Its operations include casting of aluminium alloys, machining castings, sheet metal cutting and forming, tube joining, component assembly, welding, brazing and soldering. It employs 150 people and has an annual sales turnover of about £5 million per year.

Prior to the study the only costs collected and identified as quality costs were the costs of operating the quality control department, expenditure on warranty, and the costs of scrap and defective products.

The research approach in this case study was to examine the company's operations against the model elements of BS 6143 [1] (the 1981 version of the Standard) and to put costs on them.

Table 6.1 Corresponding sections in BS 6143 and ASQC categorization of quality-related cost elements

BS 6143	ASQC	Elements
A1	1, 1a, 1b	Quality control and process control engineering
A2	2	Design and develop control equipment
A3	3	Quality planning by others
A4	–	Production equipment for quality – maintenance and calibration
A5	–	Test and inspection equipment – maintenance and calibration
A6	1a*	Supplier quality assurance
A7	4	Training
A8	5	Administration, audit, improvement
B1	2	Laboratory acceptance testing
B2	1, 3	Inspection and test
B3	4	In-process inspection (non-inspectors)
B4	5	Set-up for inspection and test
B5	6, 17	Inspection and test materials
B6	7, 8, 16	Product quality audits
B7	10	Review of test and inspection data
B8	11	On-site performance testing
B9	12	Internal testing and release
B10	13	Evaluation of materials and spares
B11	15	Data processing, inspection and test reports
	14	As A4
	9	As A5
C1	1	Scrap
C2	2	Rework and repair
C3	3	Trouble shooting, defect analysis
C4	4	Reinspect, retest
C5	5	Scrap and rework: fault of supplier
C6	6	Modification permits and concessions
C7	7	Downgrading
D1	1	Complaints
D2	2	Product service: liability
D3	3	Products returned or recalled
D4	4	Returned material repair
D5	5, 6, 7, 8	Warranty replacement

*Supplier quality assurance prior to order placement only.

The company's quality costs for the first quarter of the current year in which the study was carried out (hereafter referred to as Year 1) were measured and then using these costs a projected quality cost report was prepared for the full year. The work was carried out in the third quarter of Year 1 by which time all the first-quarter transactions and accounting were complete.

In this study a deliberately ingenuous approach was adopted to try to ensure that all the major obstacles to the collection of quality costs in the company were discovered. Before attempting to gather costs, knowledge of the company's operations and practices was gained by studying the company's procedures and reports, supplemented by discussions with staff from quality control, inspection, personnel, work study, production and accounts departments.

Attempts were then made to detect and measure costs against each of the cost elements listed in the BS 6143 guide [1] (the 1981 version of the Standard). A list of abbreviated elements, their coding and the corresponding coding used by the ASQC [2] is shown in Table 6.1. Each element given in Table 6.1 is fully defined in the body of this chapter.

It should be noted that some revision of the cost elements has been made in Part 2 of the 1990 version of BS 6143 [3].

6.2 Company quality control and accounting systems

The company, which is an approved supplier to the Ministry of Defence, has a comprehensive quality manual clearly setting out the responsibilities of quality, production, engineering and other personnel for quality-related matters. The manual contains no reference to quality costs other than warranty. There was, however, a clear acknowledgement of the existence of quality costs in the company.

The company accounting system divides the company into 21 indirect cost centres, covering its manufacturing facilities. There are also 188 financial codes, of which, apart from the routine administrative codes applied to the quality control cost centre, only sales of scrap material, indirect materials, inspection equipment, research materials and warranty repairs were readily recognizable as being quality related. Another potential source of quality cost information – labour bookings – was equally disappointing, having only 'defective material' as an obviously quality-related code, though it was learned later that bookings to 'prototype' might also contain some quality costs. The accounts department does, however, produce a monthly scrap report analysed across production cost centres and displaying material, labour and overhead costs.

It is fair to say that so far as quality-related costs are concerned the accounting system lacked sophistication and the availability of data failed to meet expectations. Some idea of the situation may be gauged from the fact that only four of the 188 financial codes referred to quality-related matters, and perhaps even more telling, there was only one labour-booking code for work concerned with defective products. As a result, the costing relied a great deal on estimates. The extent of estimation was such that only 50% of the total quality costs were derived from data specifically noted in accounts under headings identifiable as being quality related.

6.3 Detection and measurement of quality-related costs

6.3.1 Prevention costs

In many ways, and as already discussed in this book, prevention is the most difficult of the categories to cost. This is because prevention activities are made up of a number of disparate elements carried out on a part-time basis by people from different departments. The cost depends heavily on estimates of apportionment of time by personnel who do not usually record how they spend their time.

A1a Quality engineering – planning the quality system and translating product design and customer quality requirements into manufacturing quality controls of materials, processes and products.

This work is carried out exclusively within the quality control department and the cumulative effort input is estimated (by the quality control manager) to be equivalent to 30% of the time of one of the senior staff* in the department.

A1b Process engineering – represents those costs associated with implementing and maintaining quality plans and procedures.

This work is also carried out exclusively within the quality control department and is estimated to take the equivalent of 30% of the time of one of the senior staff in the department.

A2 Design and development of quality measurement and control equipment.

The cost sources for this element are (1) staff time inputs from the quality control department and production engineering department, estimated to be 5% of a senior member in each case; (2) research and development work carried out at headquarters on behalf of the local factory; and (3) (possibly) charges collected under the financial code for research materials.
It is worth noting that in discussions with company personnel a view was expressed that it would be more appropriate to include this element under the category of appraisal instead of prevention.

A3 Quality planning by functions other than the quality control department.

BS 6143 lists possible inputs from laboratory, manufacturing,

---

*In the interests of confidentiality of salary information, and because some tasks may be undertaken by any or all of the three senior people in the quality control department, a 'senior man' with, at the time of the study, an employment cost of £10 000 per year was invented.

engineering and sales personnel, none of which applies in this company, according to the quality control manager.

A4   Calibration and maintenance of production equipment used to evaluate quality.

The only item of expenditure under this heading is the calibration and maintenance of pressure gauges, estimated at half a man-day per month. It is arguable that maintenance of water baths used for detection of leaks in soldered joints should be included under this heading or indeed that this type of expenditure properly belongs in the appraisal category as is recommended by the ASQC.

It is worth noting here that whilst, overall, there is generally close agreement between BS 6143 and the ASQC on the content and categorization of cost elements, the British Standard classifies calibration and maintenance of production equipments used to evaluate quality (element A4) and maintenance and calibration of test and inspection equipment (element A5) as prevention activities, whereas the ASQC regards them as appraisal activities (appraisal elements 14 and 9 respectively).

A5   Maintenance and calibration of test and inspection equipment.

Sources of cost data for this element are (1) the financial code for indirect materials – inspection equipment; (2) invoices for calibration services from outside the company; and (3) staff time input, estimated as being 5% of a senior man's time.

It is noteworthy that a £12 000 capital investment in calibration equipment has reduced the cost of purchased calibration services from approximately £7500 per year to £2000–£3000 per year.

A6   Supplier assurance.

The costs of this element are wholly within the quality control department. The involvement of purchasing and material control staff with suppliers or subcontractors is not seen as incurring any quality-related costs. The staff time input from the quality control department is estimated to be 8% of a senior man.

A7   Quality training.

Quality-related training is not identified separately within the training function of the personnel department. Training schedules for new workers emphasize the necessity for doing work of the correct quality but no specific quality training is given. In the quality control department an estimated 2% of a senior man's time is devoted to quality training activities.

A8   Administration, audit, improvement.

Administration costs such as travel, telephones, post, printing, etc. are collected under individual financial codes but not by cost centre. Costs could be allocated on proportional bases but it has been found that the allocations vary widely, depending on the basis used, so that it is difficult to arrive at an agreed equitable allocation, much less an accurate one. Depreciation costs of the capital assets of the quality control department are available.

Auditing and improvement costs, mostly incurred within the quality control department, are estimated as equivalent to 15% of a senior man's time. It is recognized that staff from other departments became involved in major audits but no estimate of their involvement, or the cost, is available.

The prevention costs and findings are summarized in Table 6.2.

6.3.2 Appraisal costs

These are defined as the costs of assessing the quality achieved and are broken down into 11 cost elements. The largest items of cost can be determined readily and accurately because they involve full-time activities by specific personnel. Less certain is the extent of involvement of quality control department senior staff and of production operators in appraisal activities.

B1   Laboratory acceptance testing (of purchased production materials).

These are costs of tests to evaluate the quality of purchased materials which become part of the final product or that are consumed during production operations. It was expected that these costs might have been readily traceable as research materials, cost transfers from headquarters services, and invoices for outside services. In the event it was found that there was no expenditure against the financial-code-designated research materials in the first quarter of Year 1 and only £56 by the design section of the engineering department in the whole year. Payments for purchased laboratory services are said to be small and infrequent. Cost transfers from headquarters (about £3000 per year) for thermal performance testing of products may contain charges which are appropriate to this element.

B2   Inspection and test (including receiving inspection).

This element covers the inspection activity from within the quality control department (but does not include testing work carried out by production operators). It is the cost of ten full-time inspectors, plus 70% of the time of a supervising foreman/manager.

B3   In-process inspection (by personnel other than inspectors).

Table 6.2 Prevention costs

Cost element	Recorded costs (£) Jan.	Feb.	Mar.	1st qtr	Projected annual cost (£)	Source	Notes
A1 Quality control and process control engineering	–	–	–	–	6000	Estimated time	
A2 Design and develop control control equipment	–	–	–	–	1000	Estimated time	Charges in respect of headquarters, R & D work not included
A3 Quality planning by others	–	–	–	–	nil	–	
A4 Production equipment for quality – maintenance and calibration	–	–	–	–	200	Estimated time	
A5 Test and inspection – maintenance and calibration	215	205	30	450	1800 2500 500	Materials External services Estimated time	External services from sub-contractor estimated '£2000–£3000 per year'
A6 Supplier quality assurance	–	–	–	–	800	Estimated time	
A7 Training	–	–	–	–	200	Estimated time	
A8 Administration, audits, improvements	–	–	–	–	1500 4000	Estimated time Capital depreciation	Travel, telephones, post, printing, etc. all collected under single cost centre
Total					18 500		
Projected annual sales turnover (%)					0.37		

This element can be complicated because in engineering manufacture operators are frequently required to carry out inspections as part of their normal work. Measurement of the cost of this kind of inspection activity is not usually practicable and probably was not intended by the committee who were responsible for preparing the Standard. However, in company 1 a major activity is testing the airtightness of soldered joints, repairing them if necessary, and retesting them. The first testing operation is inextricably linked with repair and retest operations, which are cost elements C2 and C4 respectively under the internal failure cost category.

The costs involved are substantial and, depending on the repair rate and the view taken about whether the 'repairs' are part of the manufacturing process or are the result of failures, the costs could be divided between the appraisal and failure categories – see C2 and C4.

In the period under review there were nine skilled workers employed full time on test and repair work. Because their work is carried out in five different manufacturing areas the amount of direct supervision their work attracts is difficult to estimate and may give a spurious impression of rigorousness which is clearly unwarranted in view of the complexities in this element. Presumably, as direct workers, test and repair men's time costs normally attract overheads.

B4 Set-up for inspection and test.

This is the payroll cost of setting up equipment or products for inspection and function testing. Whilst it is known that time is booked in the machine shop for set-up and test of machines, and that costs must be incurred in setting up products for thermal testing, it is probably not worth separating them out. The element is clearly intended for industries which manufacture large, heavy or complex products for which it can be a substantial cost item.

B5 Inspection and test materials (i.e. materials consumed or destroyed in the control of quality).

Material usages for this purpose are small and most costs have been included under element A5. Material usages arising from destructive test (e.g. temperature cones) are included in the company's scrap costs.

B6 Product quality audits.

These are estimated to take up 2% of the time of a foreman/manager in the quality control department.

B7 Review of test and inspection data.

If, as believed, this means checking that all the inspection and test schedules (usually associated with heavy engineering projects) have been met, the practice of 100% final inspection and test of all products obviates the need for regular review of test and inspection data before release of the product for shipment.

B8   Field (on-site) performance testing – costs incurred in testing for product acceptance on customers' premises.

This activity, which may involve representatives of the quality control and design departments, is not large and neither staff time nor travelling expenses incurred is separated out.

B9   Internal testing and release – the cost of setting up and in-house testing of the complete product for customer acceptance.

Such work would normally be covered under B3 in company 1. Occasionally special arrangements may be made for a customer to witness tests. The level of staff involvement in this activity is estimated to be 2% of a senior man's time.

B10   Evaluation of site material (field stock) and spare parts – the costs of evaluation, testing or inspection of site material, resulting from engineering changes, storage conditions or other suspected problems.

Because much of the company's production is made for stock by distributors and users there is often a considerable delay between manufacture and the product going into service. Hence problems arise from deterioration during storage, changes to specifications, etc. It is estimated that attention to these problems takes up to 5% of a senior man's time.

B11   Data processing inspection and test reports – the costs incurred in accumulating and processing test and inspection data used in evaluation work.

The bulk of this work is carried out within the quality control department and involves data from service centres as well as the manufacturing operation. It occupies an estimated 20% of the time of a senior man in the department. The cost of accumulating data by production personnel and inspectors is not known.

The results of the examination of appraisal costs are shown in Table 6.3

6.3.3 Internal failure costs
These are defined as the costs arising wthin the manufacturing organization of the failure to achieve the quality specified (before transfer of

Table 6.3 Appraisal costs

Cost element		Recorded costs Jan.	Feb.	Mar.	1st qtr	Projected annual costs (£)	Source	Notes
B1	Laboratory acceptance testing	–	–	–	–	–	–	Possibly £3000
B2	Inspection and test	–	–	–	–	80 000 7 000	– Estimated time	Employment cost of full-time inspectors Supervisor/manager part-time
B3	In-process inspection (non-inspectors)	–	–	–	–	67 500	–	Full-time test and repair men; overheads not included; including overheads £396 000
B4	Set-up for inspection and test	–	–	–	–	–	–	Not applicable
B5	Inspection and test materials	–	–	–	–	–	–	Included under A5 and C1
B6	Product quality audits	–	–	–	–	200	Estimated time	
B7	Review of test and inspection data	–	–	–	–	–	–	Not applicable
B8	On-site performance tests	–	–	–	–	200	Estimated time	
B9	Internal test and release	–	–	–	–	200	Estimated time	
B10	Evaluation of materials and spares	–	–	–	–	500	Estimated time	
B11	Data processing	–	–	–	–	2 000	Estimated time	
Total						157 600		
Projected annual sales turnover (%)						3.14		May be much higher; See notes at B1 and B3 above

ownership to the customer). The major items of cost are scrap and rework. The cost elements comprising internal failure costs, according to BS 6143, are as follows:

C1 Scrap – all scrap losses incurred in the course of meeting quality requirements. This element includes only that scrap arising through the fault of the manufacturer; that which is the fault of a supplier is included under element C5.

Costs are generated from inspection/rejection reports and standard costs. They comprise the cost of materials and direct labour to the point of scrapping. The direct labour costs include overhead charges. Inclusion of overheads in this way has the effect of inflating some failure costs relative to other quality costs which do not attract overheads. It is not clear whether allowance is made for parts recovered from scrapped products.

An interesting and expensive source of scrap which is quality-related arises at company 1. It is that scrap which is described as 'natural wastage' and arises mainly from setting-up and offcuts. The offcuts arise from stamping out components from metal tubes, etc. Clearly every effort is made to minimize such wastage, but some is unavoidable. Similarly, although scrap materials are used whenever possible in setting up machines there is inevitably some waste when good new material has to be used for the final checks before producing components for use. The value of such materials could only be construed as quality costs if the amount of scrap produced in this way could be shown to be greater than was necessary.

Non-ferrous scrap is segregated into various categories (copper, brass, clear, tinned, etc.) and sold. Despite the BS 6143 guidance to the contrary, the income from these sales should not be deducted from the costs of scrapping products because (1) it makes the quality performance appear to be better than it really is; (2) the type and quantity of scrap sold at a particular time may bear no relationship to the current output; and (3) the inclusion of 'natural wastage' in the scrap sold would, in effect, subsidize non-conforming product. It is interesting to note that the income from sales of scrap in the first quarter is approximately equal to the materials' value of products scrapped in the same period.

Staff time input from the quality control department is estimated as 10% of a senior man's time and there is some input from the accounts department in preparing cost data. However, in view of the fact that scrap costs include overheads, it would be wrong to add on these costs.

C2 Rework and repair – the cost incurred in meeting quality requirements where material can be restored for use.

As mentioned earlier under B3, the apportionment of costs
between elements B2, C2 and C4 is complicated because of the
test and repair activity. However, irrespective of the outcome of
any consideration given to such apportionment, there are other
costs which clearly should be included under this element. The
company's quality manual prescribes a system by which the direct
hours and issue of the necessary excess materials is formally recorded and passed to the accounts department. So far as is known,
these costs are not formally reported and the best information that
could be gleaned was the half-time involvement of a welder on
castings and the record of hours claimed under the heading of
'defective materials'. In order to be consistent with the accounting
practice used to calculate the cost of producing scrap, it is of course
necessary to add overhead charges to these costs.

C3 Troubleshooting or defect/failure analysis (to determine causes).

This work is carried out within the quality control department
and is estimated to take 10% of the time of a senior man in the
department.

C4 Reinspection, retesting (of products which had failed previously).

As discussed under B3 and C2 above, the involvement of test and
repair workers in the production process complicates apportionment in this heading. Reinspection and retesting of rerouted
rework is not identified separately from first inspection and tests.
Because initial failure rates can be as high as 50% (albeit with
easily repairable minor defects) the costs of the activities under
this element could be fairly large.

C5 Scrap and rework; fault of supplier; downtime.

Suppliers are expected to reimburse the full purchase price of any
supplies which are unusable owing to the supplier's fault. Any
other costs incurred up to the point of scrapping are not recovered.
On the matter of rework, it is either carried out by the supplier
or by the company at the supplier's expense. On some occasions
attempted rework of faulty supplies may cause some lost time,
materials or throughput. Overall there is little net cost to the
company, but records are worth keeping for supplier assessment
purposes.

C6 Modifications, permits and concessions – the costs of time spent
reviewing products, designs and specifications.

Modifications are usually covered by concessions – usually from the engineering department or (occasionally) from customers. No estimates of the time or costs involved were obtained from the engineering department, but it was learned from the accounts department that there is a substantial monthly design charge, much of which could be related to design changes. The input from the quality control department is estimated to be 10% of the time of a senior member of the department.

C7   Downgrading.

It is not the practice of the company to sell 'seconds' at a reduced price.

These considerations and findings on internal failure cost are summarized in Table 6.4.

6.3.4 External failure costs

These are defined as the costs arising outside the manufacturing organization of the failure to achieve the quality specified (after transfer of ownership to the customer). Interpretation of the definition is not as straightforward as it appears, inasmuch that (1) the point of transfer of ownership is not unequivocally defined; and (2) in the case of this company's products, the warranty period may not be initiated until several years after the sale of the product to the customer.

D1   Complaints administration – the costs of administration of those complaints which are due to quality defects.

Complaints being handled by the manufacturing company (as distinct from the distribution service and agency outlets) are dealt with wholly within the quality control department. It is estimated that the time spent on such matters is 5% of the time of a senior member of the department's staff.

D2   Product or consumer service; product liability.

Costs arising within the manufacturing company are likely to be included under D1 above.

D3   Handling and accounting of products rejected or recalled.

Costs of these are not measured or estimated. They are probably negligible.

D4   Returned material repair.

Repair work is carried out under one cost centre and covers (1) work which is chargeable back to the customer; (2) work done under warranty; and (3) repairs carried out free of charge. It is

Table 6.4 Internal failure costs

Cost element	Recorded costs (£)				Projected annual costs (£)	Source	Notes
	Jan.	Feb.	Mar.	1st qtr			
C1 Scrap	10 885	11 945	15 710	38 540	154 160	Accounts	Scrap valuation includes overheads
C2 Rework and repair	6 700	7 584	7 363	21 647	86 588	'Defective material' hours	
					15 000	Estimated time	Welder part time plus overheads
					1 000	Estimated time	Supervisor/manager part time
C3 Trouble shooting and defect analysis	–	–	–	–	1 000	Estimated time	
C4 Reinspect, retest	–	–	–	–	–	–	Included under B3
C5 Scrap and rework suppliers' fault	–	–	–	–	–	–	Negligible net cost
C6 Modification permits, concessions	–	–	–	–	1 000	Estimated time	Assumes all 'design charges' are related to modifications
					33 000	Engineering department	
C7 Downgrading	–	–	–	–	–	–	Not applicable
Total					291 748		Without overheads this total reduces to £106 000
Projected turnover (%)					5.8		

important here to distinguish between (2) and (3). Work done under warranty is work relating to products which have failed in service whilst under warranty (other warranty costs are included under D5 by virtue of work carried out by retail service outlets). Work done free of charge on products returned by customers is work relating to products which failed on test or were damaged on receipt or corroded, etc. It is this latter cost which is to be collected under this element. It is identified in the accounts as 'Company Liability'. The quality control department staff effort input to this activity is inseparable from that going into element D5.

D5   Warranty replacement – the costs of replacing products which have failed within the warranty period.

Charges arise from several different sources: (1) payments made to service centres for repairs carried out under warranty; (2) replacement products issued free of charge to service centres or customers in exchange for failed products which are repairable; and (3) staff time input dealing with warranty claims and pay-ments – 65% of a quality engineer's time.

Whilst simple in principle, the actual method of achieving the objective of satisfying customers may render the collection of costs difficult. Some customers deal directly with the factory and faulty product may be repaired and returned to the customer at a certain cost, or they may be replaced in the stock by stripping and refur-bishing the returned unit, but at a different cost. Service centres are recompensed at agreed rates for warranty repair work, but the same rates do not appear to apply to similar repairs carried out at the factory. Replacement units issued by service centres when a faulty unit is irrepairable are billed at the service centre stock valuation, which, of course, is far higher than the factory issue price. Free-of-charge replacements of products found to be faulty before going into service are more straightforward but the valu-ation and crediting of the returned damaged products is unclear.

The external failure costs are summarized in Table 6.5.

6.4 Discussion of findings

In carrying out the costing exercise points have been raised and dis-cussed briefly in the context of the element or category. It is intended here to discuss each category in the broader context of the cost collection exercise as a whole.

Table 6.5 External failure costs

Cost element		Recorded costs (£) Jan. Feb. Mar. 1st qtr	Projected annual costs (£)	Source	Notes
D1	Complaints administration	– – – –	500	Estimated time	
D2	Product service, liability	– – – –	–	–	Covered under D1 and D5
D3	Returned product handling and accounting	– – – –	–	–	Included in D4
D4	Returned products' repair	2 896 2 816 3 709 9 421	37 684	Accounts	Inclusion of overheads uncertain
D5	Warranty replacement	1 744 1 612 2 217 5 573	22 292 6 500	Accounts Estimated time	Uncertain if all costs included
	Total		66 976		
	Projected annual sales turnover (%)		1.34		

6.4.1 Prevention costs

In a small company, where the many disparate preventive activities are
not sufficiently large to occupy the whole or even a large proportion of
an employee's time, it is necessary to record or estimate the proportions
of time spent on each activity in order to obtain a prevention cost
analysis. Estimates of the proportions of time spent on various activities
tend to be highly subjective and may be 'average' or 'typical' observations not necessarily specifically relating to the period under review.
It has been found in this case study and the others discussed in the
chapters which follow that estimates tend to be based on medium- or
long-term experiences and may not reflect current experiences. Furthermore, estimates tend not to change. Once a considered view has been
arrived at the estimator tends to stick with it.

In the present instance some 55% of the prevention cost is derived
from estimated time coupled with an average employment cost. With
the foregoing remarks in mind, this might be expected to yield a fairly
inaccurate estimate of prevention costs, especially when coupled to
uncertainties about charges in respect of research and development
work at headquarters and other outside services. However, when it is
realized that the whole prevention activity cost amounts to only around
5% of the estimated total quality-related cost and less than 0.4% of
projected annual sales turnover the case for accurate time apportionment and costing takes on a different perspective. Furthermore, if one
takes the view that only those costs which are subject to change, or are
sensitive to some business parameter, should be collected and analysed
accurately, there seems little point in gathering detailed information
about how much time people devote to various prevention activities.
Thus, it is important to keep cost elements or categories in perspective
and not agonize over the accuracy of minor cost elements in the prevention category. On the other hand, over the quality-related cost spectrum
the full-time activity of three employees at a total employment cost of
about £30 000 per year is being apportioned by subjective estimates. It
may be that the size of activity is worth monitoring by recording the
time spent on the major elements of quality activities. It is suggested
that noting half-day increments once weekly against those topics which
this study has shown to be the most important would adequately meet
the need.

As already noted, for the purpose of ascribing costs to staff time,
whilst maintaining confidentiality of individual salaries, and owing to
the fact that some of the activities may involve any or all of the senior
staff in the quality control department (i.e. quality control manager,
quality control engineer, quality control foreman), a hypothetical 'senior
man' was invented. If further justification is needed, it is suggested

that the validity of the assumption is at least as great as the validity of completeness of the underlying data.

6.4.2 Appraisal costs

Clearly the costs of inspection and testing are far greater than all the other appraisal costs put together. Indeed some of the elements listed in BS 6143 attract no costs at all, and several others which together account for less than 10% of a manager's time might usefully be combined. In fact, apart from charges incurred for laboratory acceptance testing, the appraisal costs are the employment costs of ten inspectors, nine test and repair men and one foreman/manager from the quality control department.

Problems of estimating apportionment of a foreman/manager's time are rather more straightforward under this category because 90% of it is divided between only two elements. None the less it is felt that it could be beneficial to record broad uses of time as suggested earlier.

Under this category two problems of definition of quality-related costs arise. The first is whether all or part of the activities of test and repair workers should be classified as being quality related, and the second is whether quality-related direct work should attract overheads for the purpose of measuring quality-related costs.

One view taken of the first problem is that the whole of the test and repair activity is a normal production cost and not a quality-related cost. Another view is that first-time test and repair is a normal production activity but that any subsequent tests and repairs are quality-related costs. Yet another view is that all the costs are quality related but that the tests are appraisal costs and the repairs are failure costs. The sum involved is the employment costs of nine workers, i.e. about £67 000 (without overheads).

The effects on quality cost distributions and ratios of omitting this cost are shown in Table 6.6. The effects of splitting the cost between production and quality, or between quality cost categories, have not been evaluated. As mentioned in Chapter 2, there is often no 'right' answer to the problem; it is a matter to be decided by people knowledgeable about the industry, the technology, the products and the processes.

The second problem, whether direct worker costs should attract overheads when measuring quality-related costs, is fundamental to the whole exercise of quality costing. The high overheads which exist in manufacturing industry can grossly distort the level and distribution of quality costs. If overheads are included, the costs of those elements involving direct workers are going to be grossly inflated in comparison with those involving indirect workers. For example, in the context of appraisal cost, assuming for the moment that the costs of test and repair direct workers are quality-related costs, the employment costs of ten full-time inspectors who are indirect workers is £80 000 whilst the cost of nine test and repair workers, including overheads, is approaching £400 000. Hence it is clearly ludicrous to include overhead charges in quality-related labour costs. In any event, because staff and indirect worker costs are being ascribed directly to quality cost elements, adding overheads to direct worker costs at the standard rate must necessarily involve some double-counting. Overheads which may sensibly accrue to quality-related costs are those included in charges from other parts of the company because they are analogous to invoice from outside companies.

The matter is discussed further below in the context of failure costs.

6.4.3 Internal failure costs

Scrap and rework charges together with design changes account for almost the whole of the cost under this category.

Although the system for collecting costs of scrap is well established,

Table 6.6 Projected annual quality costs and cost ratios: effects of overheads and 'test and repair' operations

Cost category		As collected	Less overhead	As collected	Less overhead	FMP†	MIG‡
				Omitting test and repair		*US survey data**	
Prevention	Projected	18 500	18 500	18 500	18 500	–	–
Appraisal	costs (£)	157 600	157 600	89 900	89 900	–	–
Internal failure		291 748	106 000	291 748	106 000	–	–
External failure		66 976	66 976	66 976	66 976	–	–
Total		534 824	349 076	467 124	281 376		
Prevention	Quality	3.4	5.3	4.0	6.5	10.5	10.3
Appraisal	costs (%)	29.5	45.1	19.3	32.0	34.5	26.0
Internal failure		54.5	30.4	62.3	37.7	39.0	43.0
External failure		12.6	19.2	14.4	23.8	16.0	20.7
Total		100	100	100	100	100	100
Prevention	Sales	0.37	0.37	0.37	0.37	0.51	0.6
Appraisal	turnover	3.14	3.14	1.8	1.8	1.67	1.5
Internal failure	(%)	5.8	2.12	5.8	2.12	1.90	2.5
External failure		1.34	1.34	1.34	1.34	0.77	1.2
Total		10.65	6.97	9.31	5.63	4.85	5.8

*Quality costs survey. *Quality*, June 1977, pp. 20–2 [4].
†FMP, fabricated metal products sector of industry.
‡MIG, manufacturing industries in general.

other costs in this category were difficult to obtain. The problem of overheads arises again, and whilst it is conceded that it is entirely appropriate for overheads to be added to direct labour charges for the purposes of stock valuations and records, it is again contended that it is not appropriate for the purpose of collecting quality-related costs. The problem arises only because of the practice of recovering overheads on a direct labour basis. If a basis of, say, units of saleable products was used, there would not be a problem. The effects on the quality cost report of omitting overheads can be seen in Table 6.6.

A noticeable feature of scrap reports is the significantly large weights of non-ferrous scrap (1 tonne per month) accruing under the heading 'natural wastage' which arises mainly from material used during set-up and from offcuts or surpluses from stamping operations. Such scrap is a production materials loss. Its value is not a quality-related cost and care must be taken that it is not counted as such. The approval of BS 6143 of the practice of deducting income from sales of scrap from scrap costs is surprising for the reasons already given under C1 earlier.

The definition of rework and repair costs is complicated by the test and repair situation as discussed earlier. Leaving aside that compli-cation, even in those cases where the definitions and procedures to

Table 6.7 Projected annual quality costs: comparison of findings on scrap, rework and warranty with US survey data

Cost category		Company 1	US survey data*	
			FMP†	MIG‡
Scrap	Projected costs (£)	154 160	–	–
Rework		101 588	–	–
Warranty		28 792	–	–
Total		284 540		
Scrap	Quality costs (%)	54.0	32.4	41.0
Rework		35.7	64.0	38.5
Warranty		10.3	3.6	20.5
Total		100	100	100
Scrap	Sales turnover (%)	3.08	3.6	3.2
Rework		2.03	7.1	3.0
Warranty		0.58	0.4	1.6
Total		5.69	11.1	7.8

*Quality costs survey. Quality, June 1977, pp. 20–2 [4].
†FMP, fabricated metal products sector of industry.
‡MIG, manufacturing industries in general.

produce rework costs appear to be straightforward, difficulty was experienced in obtaining them. The figures quoted in Table 6.6 were the best that could be obtained at the time but they appear to be very low in comparison with other reported data (see Tables 6.6 and 6.7).

Similarly no firm data were available for the costs of modifications, concessions and the general impact of design engineering on quality-related costs. Without more detailed enquiries there is no way of gauging whether the figure quoted in Table 6.6 is anywhere near correct. It would appear that the costs to be included under this element appear to be very specific to the industry/company.

In the context of internal failure costs it is interesting to speculate whether the true economics surrounding the scrap or rework decision are known for each product under different conditions of output rate, urgency of delivery, materials supply, etc., or whether the decisions are really made in the light of engineering knowledge and experience.

6.4.4 External failure costs

The major costs incurred under this heading are for repair of products which have been returned by customers because they were found to be faulty before being put into service, and replacement of products which have failed in service during the warranty period.

Although superficially it should be a simple matter to determine the magnitude of these costs, in practice it is complicated by some business and accounting practices. The systems are described under D4 and D5. Examples of the complications which arise in ascertaining quality costs are replacement of a defective unit from stock and replenishing the stock by refurbishing (as distinct from repairing) the faulty unit, and the obscuration of in-house warranty work carried out in the repair section of the factory. However, the figures quoted in Table 6.5 are as supplied by the accounts department and have, presumably, been properly disentangled.

6.5 Presentation and uses of quality-related costs

The only presentation and uses of quality-related costs in company 1 are the monthly reporting of the quality control department costs for budgetary control purposes and reporting of gross costs of scrap and warranty in management accounts. Although ratios are used as performance indicators in some aspects of the business, gross values are preferred. Quality costs do not feature in any of the ratios used. These typically involve measures of labour, sales and manufacturing cost. Costs do not appear to feature specifically in the day-to-day decisions about quality matters though it must be said that there is a very cost-conscious atmosphere about the factory. On the other hand, dealing with warranty claims is a very cost-oriented activity, the basic documentation for which is a list of product applications, normal warranty limits, exceptions, warranty reimbursement costs, and agreed labour rates for agencies and service centres.

6.6 Overall review and comparison with other data

Table 6.6 summarizes the costs collected in this study and shows their distribution and ratio to projected annual sales turnover (£5 million). The table also shows distributions and ratios determined from an American survey [4] of quality-related costs. Although the industries surveyed were very diverse, and even the fabricated metal products sector of industry covers a wide range of products, it is interesting to observe some of the comparisons.

Clearly, omitting the test and repair costs and overheads from the company's quality costs yields distributions and ratios similar to those found in the American survey which, although the details of the computation of the American data are not known, and it would be unwise to infer too much from the comparison, suggests that even with all the limitations discussed above the costs determined in this exercise are not grossly in error and the company performance may be close to average.

Table 6.7 shows the company performance compared with that of another set of respondents to the American survey. This set of respondents measured only failure costs under the headings of scrap, rework and warranty. Again, without reading too much into the figures, it appears that the company's failure costs may be lower than might be expected, but there is also a suggestion that estimates of rework costs may be low and that the distribution of cost between scrap and rework is abnormal. However, it cannot be stressed too strongly that these are merely interesting observations and are not a basis for conclusions leading to any kind of action.

The costs are also shown graphically in Figures 6.1 and 6.2 These show clearly that the major costs are internal failure costs and that 95% of costs are ascribable to seven of 28 elements. It appears unlikely, even allowing for the uncertainties, errors and lack of information, that the picture grossly misrepresents the situation in the company. It also puts into proper perspective the subdivision of categories into many elements and the pursuit of accuracy in costing minor elements. A feature of the analysis was that one could readily obtain marked changes in proportions of sales annual turnover and of quality costs depending on the view taken about inclusion of test and repair work as a quality cost, and of overheads.

Aspects of quality costs not uncovered by the BS 6143 checklist

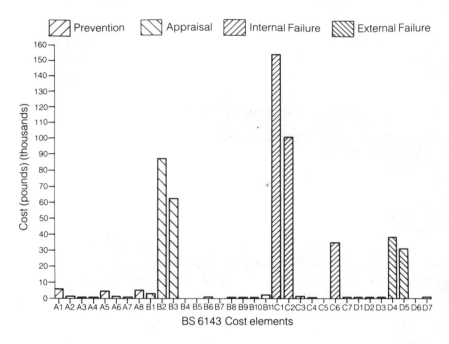

Figure 6.1 Quality costs.

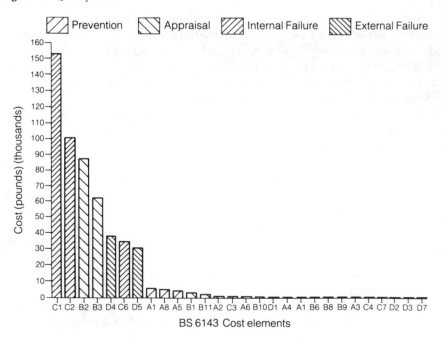

Figure 6.2 Quality costs.

approach, but which were revealed in discussions with company personnel, are an arbitrary 10% excess materials allowed for 'headers' of casting moulds, and a 2.5% allowance for scrap in computing product costs. It is also normal practice to allow for losses by planning for 3% more production than is required.

6.7 Miscellaneous points arising from the study

Although it is believed that most of the major quality-related cost sources have been identified and reasonable estimates of the cost magnitudes of the different elements have been made, it is worth touching briefly on a few of the difficulties met with in trying to evaluate costs. These may be of value to other quality cost collectors. It is accepted and understood that various practices in a company come about for good and sensible reasons, nevertheless some practices complicated and hampered the exercise to the extent that some costs were never properly resolved. These include the following:

• Use of different words and headings for the same thing in different departments.
• Different departments using different dates for the same transaction of activity.
• Use of calendar months in some departments versus week numbers and accounting periods in others.
• Loose use of the word 'scrap' to mean or include rejected products, production waste and rework.
• Retesting after repair booked as testing.
• Unmeasured work booked to 'prototype'.
• There is a minimum bonus rate for skilled workers doing non-productive tasks. Hence their time is booked to high-bonus codes irrespective of the task. Unskilled workers book to the correct code.
• There is only one rework code. It is sometimes used for booking time spent on inspection and sorting, thus combining appraisal costs with failure costs.
• A worker may properly book time to several cost centres but their 'home' cost centre carries the cost.
• Some costs lose their identity because bonus claims of the same value are lumped together for wage calculation purposes.
• Some different types of claims are combined because of an eight-column limit on the computer analysis display and print-out.
• Internal informal reporting does not always distinguish clearly between free-of-charge repairs and warranty costs.

References

1. BS 6143 (1981) *The Determination and Use of Quality-Related Costs*, British Standards Institution, London.
2. ASQC Quality Costs Committee (1974) *Quality Costs – What and How*, American Society for Quality Control, Milwaukee WI.
3. BS 6143: Part 2 (1990) *Guide to the Economics of Quality: Prevention, appraisal and failure model*, British Standards Institution, London.
4. Anon (1977) Quality cost survey. *Quality*, 20–2.

7
Case study, company 2

7.1 Introduction

Company 2 is engaged in the manufacture of ancillary equipment for reciprocating engines used mainly for powering trucks and cars. it produces some 300 000 units per year in a variety of sizes and configurations to suit different applications. It makes a precision product which operates under difficult service conditions. The manufacturing operations are essentially machining, forming, assembly and test and are carried out on a two-shift small-to-medium batch production basis. It is one of six manufacturing divisions and has an annual sales turnover of some £72 million and is part of a diversfied major American corporation.

The fact that its customers are few in number, technically expert, commercially powerful and extremely competitive has considerable ramifications for the company, especially as engine and vehicle manufacturers feel that poor performance from the company's products may adversely affect their own reputations in the marketplace. Company 2's products feature strongly in the customers' promotion of the image and performance of their goods. It is probably true also that the rapid rate of growth of the market means that customer loyalty has not yet become established to the point of being a major factor in the placing of orders. Add to this ownership by a company with its roots in aerospace technology, and international competition from both within and outside the company, and the result is a dynamic operation with an aggressive attitude to continuous quality improvement. The managing director makes an analogy between poor quality and friction in machines – one should be trying always to eliminate them. But quality was not its only crusade. Quality topics have to compete with manufacturing system development, advanced machining systems, just-in-time, energy-saving and other cost-saving topics for money and resources.

The company's earliest attempts to collect quality costs were very rudimentary – scrap and rejects in the plant, and warranty claims from customers. The availability of quality cost information has developed with the quality system itself, such that many important quality costs are now available on a weekly computer print-out. In the beginning the company used the quality and costing systems of the parent company in an informal manner. It took the combined pressures of a sharp increase in production requirements and a particularly exacting customer to force the company into formalizing its methods of working. It was a traumatic exercise in which the company looked closely at what it was doing. It found that making people do what they really should be doing was not easy. However, it resulted – among other things – in a five-year vision, strategy, objectives and plan for the development of total quality management, the formation of a quality assurance (as opposed to inspection) department with a senior manager in charge, and considerable capital expenditure on quality-related equipment. The quality system has continued to be developed such that current emphasis is on vendor development and on providing the best total value to the customer in terms of overall excellence of performance and quality, not just in terms of hardware delivered but also in terms of total product and service over the complete life cycle of the product. Tangible evidence of the developments is seen in the regular detailed reporting of quality and cost information to functional managers and of scrap and reject costs, by departments, to shopfloor workers. The conference sessions also indicate the importance attached to quality matters with cost-reduction meetings held monthly and product quality review meetings daily.

Whilst the company acknowledges the general usefulness of quality-related costs in everyday decision-making, it had at the time a deeper purpose for establishing a rigorous system for collecting and presenting costs. It also had a considerable obstacle to overcome to reach its ultimate objectives. The company manufactures for a rapidly expanding market and the parent company intended to expand the manufacturing facilities at some of its sites. Thus, the six manufacturing divisions are in competition with each other for a large capital investment. Company 2 is confident that its quality record is superior to that of its group competitors and wishes to devise a rigorous system of cost definition, collection and presentation to be adopted by all the manufacturing divisions so that its superiority shows. The obstacle to this objective is that the headquarters manufacturing division uses a different cost system to the other competing divisions. The headquarters division uses a project-costing system whilst the others all use standard-costing systems. A further objective was to try to use costs to indicate how, where and when to invest in prevention.

The company was indeed successful in demonstrating to its parent company that it was competitive in terms of quality, cost and delivery, and additional capital investment has been made available to the site in question.

7.2 Identification of sources of quality costs

In this second case study a more flexible approach was taken to the identification of sources of quality costs than in the first case study. Briefly, the approach used was to study the quality and costing functions in action, without prejudice, and to make comparisons later. As a first step, the company's systems and procedures manual was closely studied for any item which might be construed as relating to quality. This generated a list of topics and questions which were raised and discussed with the quality manager and other staff as seemed appropriate. A similar exercise was then carried out on the company's costing system. Only when these studies were complete was any attempt made to make comparison with BS 6143 and, later, to draw up a quality-related cost report.

7.3 Sources of cost identified from systems and procedures

Copies of the company's systems manual are held by departmental heads who have the responsibility of ensuring that all their staff are aware of new or revised systems which affect the running of the respective department. The systems are drawn up by a full-time systems administrator in conjunction with the heads of the departments involved in operating the system. Each system sets down the objective and the procedure to be followed. The titles and position of personnel responsible for actions in the procedure is indicated together with the appropriate form reference numbers. Managers with responsibility for operating the systems are signatories to the system. Thus, the company view of what are quality-related systems is immediately apparent because the quality manager is a signatory to them. The following systems were identified as being quality related:

1. goods receiving – production material;
2. goods receiving – tooling, gauges, etc.;
3. internal quality control and assurance procedures;
4. manufacturing quality review;
5. coding for scrap parts;

6.   product specification, serial numbers, etc.;
7.   suppliers' sample approval;
8.   assembly release;
9.   disposal of in-process scrap;
10. in-process scrap control;
11. inspection test and product stripdown;
12. request for tool store service;
13. engineering concessions;
14. engineering orders;
15. engineering instructions;
16. release of work to manufacturing areas;
17. outside processing of components.

It might have been expected that control of engineering and manufacturing specifications, tool control, foundry scrap for set-up, and issue of replacement parts for assembly would also have borne the quality manager's signature, but this was not the case.

Amongst the topics and questions generated from the survey of procedures and systems were those shown below. They are given here as examples of issues which have to be resolved in a quality cost collection exercise and are aspects to be considered by quality cost collectors.

- Is the preparation of systems and procedures in itself a quality-related activity? (Especially as no fewer than 17 of the company's 50 procedures related to topics that are clearly quality oriented.)
- Can quality awareness by stores personnel (e.g. by stock rotation, suitable storage, careful handling, etc.) be considered as a quality cost?
- Among the codes to which direct workers may book non-productive time are some (e.g. sorting) which may involve them in quality-related work without it being apparent from their job cards.
- When it is not possible to identify the department responsible for the loss of hours, the rework/excess work account must be specified.
- The time spent on the rectification of supplier faults is booked to the materials control department (presumably with the intention of recovering the cost from the supplier) but it is given a quality tag by noting the inspection reject report number on the time return.
- A system which requires all systems to be audited periodically is not itself classified as a quality-oriented system – at least as judged by the affiliations of the authorizing signatories.
- Instructions relating to the receipt and handling of products for service and repair do not suggest these activities are quality related.
- Is the movement of inward goods to a bonded area to await inspection a quality-related activity?

- Are the costs of purchasing and accounts departments dealing with rejected supplies quality related?
- The process of gauging may cause quality-related costs to arise. If gauging frequency is low it may be achieved within the standard machining time. If it is high, it may interfere with the rate of production. How should the costs of gauging be classified in these two cases?
- The necessity for resetting machines is a quality-related matter. Is downtime for machine resetting a quality cost?
- What is the cost of machine downtime?
- What are the economics of improved machine capability versus the higher capital cost?
- The time at which a machine is stopped by an inspector (on the grounds of product non-conformance) is logged but the time of restarting is not.
- Testing of products under simulated operating conditions is the responsibility of the quality assurance department.
- The disposition of rejected components or assemblies involves personnel from outside the quality assurance department in unmeasured quality activities (e.g. marking and segregating scrap, defining rework, scheduling rework on to the shopfloor).
- Codes for scrap and reworkable parts contain definitions such that the value of the scrapped part may not be a quality-related cost (e.g. parts no longer usable due to customer and/or engineering changes or errors).
- Some definitions of codes for scrap and reworkable parts imply that the economics of reworking and of salvaging parts are known and are the basis of the decisions whether to scrap or rework components.
- Non-working time codes on operator job cards contain two codes which are quality-related: (1) stopped by inspection and (2) waiting first-off and others. Are the costs quantifiable and, if so, are they appraisal costs? It should be noted that reasons for non-working not covered by other codes is added to (2) above.
- Excess codes cover rework and extra operations and are generally regarded as quality costs. However, one code – extra machining operations – may be used for reasons unconnected with quality (e.g. poor tooling).
- Drawing and print control are usual activities in engineering manufacture and are a quality safeguard. Is a quality-related cost incurred in this activity?
- Completed parts are stored in a clean area and protected from dust settlement. Can these precautions be considered as quality-related costs?

- Is the use of expensive packing materials to protect the product in transit a quality-related cost?
- Materials and contracts personnel get involved in dealing with non-conforming items received from overseas suppliers.
- The process route traveller requires the point of scrapping to be noted on the form.
- What are the costs incurred due to order-splitting because of rejection? There appears to be some difficulty in getting a disposition decision before the next processing operation.
- The quality assurance department is involved in agreeing fixed manufacturing costs. Does this include the opportunity cost of losing capacity during machine set-up?
- Although primary responsibility for engineering concession authorization lies with the product engineering department, quality assurance and production control departments become heavily involved.
- When traceability of parts released on concession is considered necessary, the sales engineering department also becomes involved and the work related to the maintenance of records increases considerably.
- Is the preparation of engineering instructions with mandatory status a quality-related cost?

7.4 Sources of costs identified from accounts ledgers

The company's costing system is the use of cost centres based on functions, cost topics and operating departments. Each cost centre is broken down into a number of cost elements each of which carries an account number and an indication of the account type (e.g. asset, liability, income or expense). It is the listing of these account numbers and titles, covering all the elements of all the cost centres, which was scrutinized for potential quality-related cost sources. This of course could only be done sensibly in the light of the knowledge gained earlier from studying the company's operations and systems.

A list of titles of accounts which it was thought might be relevant to the quality cost collection exercise and some other pertinent points uncovered are shown below. Again these may be helpful to people undertaking a quality costing exercise.

- Provision for stock loss.
- Obsolescence.
- Laboratory equipment.
- Office furniture and fittings.
- Product component cleaning machinery.
- Provision for warranty payments.

- PAYE, superannuation, holiday pay, etc.
- Product transfers to other divisions.
- Resale of refurbished products.
- Spares.
- Transfer of spares to other divisions.
- Repairs.
- After-sales service.
- Refurbishing returned units.
- Rework.
- Scrap materials.
- Scrap sales.
- Warranty costs.
- Reject materials.
- Stock loss provision.
- Redundant stock scrapped.
- Customer exception costs.
- Depreciation.
- Administration (salaries, travel, etc.).
- Product technology.
- Repairs to machinery and equipment.
- Operating supplies.
- Field test supplies.
- Quality assurance department.
- Customer engineering department.
- Product support department.
- Production department.
- Works engineering department.
- Manufacturing engineering department.
- Industrial engineering department.
- Standard costs derived from materials and labour costs and the recovery of overheads include an allowance of 5% for scrap losses.
- Scrap is valued at the materials cost plus half the direct labour and overhead costs which would have been incurred if the item had been processed to completion.
- Scrap sales records include allowance made to the customer on returned product which cannot be repaired.
- Rework costs include the cost of sorting rejected batches.
- The value of products returned by customers before being put into service is collected in a separate account and added to rework costs.
- Special accounts are set up to deal with abnormal warranty situations.
- 'Customer exception costs' are costs of the company's quality assurance staff based at a customer's works dealing with an exceptional problem.

- Suppliers are debited with the value of faulty goods supplied.
- There is, possibly, some double-counting taking place when items are scrapped after rework.
- Rework costs do not include overheads.
- Not all the sort and rework claims are accepted by the accounts department. Owing to the fact that rework and other non-productive hours of direct workers are deducted from total hours before production efficiency is calculated based on the remaining hours, it may be in the production department's interest to claim as many non-productive hours as it can.

The company operates over a thousand active accounts across 33 cost centres. Hence the 30 or so accounts identified as possibly being directly relevant to a cost collection exercise seem but a small fraction of the total. However, it must be pointed out that the same account titles recur under different cost centres. It is also the case that there is a proliferation of cost centres, especially in those activities closest to the manufacturing operation. Since cost centres suffice for departments/functions such as administration, finance, personnel, purchasing, production control, sales administration, customer engineering, etc., works engineering, manufacturing engineering and quality assurance have four cost centres each (one administration and one for each factory site), and production has five cost centres through which to control its costs. In the case of the quality assurance department, four cost centres for 35 personnel (at least 80% of whose costs must be remuneration) is surely an accounting extravagance. However, it is by no means unusual for there to be closer scrutiny and analysis of costs the nearer one gets to the manufacturing operation. Perhaps this is because the manufacturing function is the easiest activity to measure.

7.5 Applicability of BS 6143 at company 2

The study also examined the applicability of BS 6143 [1] (the 1981 version of the Standard) in the company. Hence, just as in company 1, the applicability of each of the elements listed in the standard was checked against the working practices in the company. However, in this case, owing to the fact that the company is American owned and that it is seeking to set up a cost reporting system which sets a style and standard acceptable to its sister companies, it made sense to keep the ASQC lists [2] and definitions in mind. In doing so differences between the ASQC and BS 6143 lists and definitions emerged and are noted. These differences are important to quality cost collectors in transnational organizations.

7.5.1 Prevention costs

Definitions of prevention costs differ slightly between the British Standard (BS) and the American Society for Quality Control (ASQC) recommendations. The principal differences are as follows.

1. The BS definition of prevention costs permits a wider range of quality-related activities (and hence costs) to be included than does the ASQC definition.
2. The BS document separates out supplier quality assurance as a specific cost element whereas the ASQC document includes only vendor surveys prior to placing an order, other dealings with vendors being classed as appraisal activities.
3. ASQC see the maintenance and calibration of test and inspection equipment used in the control of quality, and production equipment used to evaluate quality, as being appraisal activities rather than prevention.

Apart from these differences there is close agreement between the two authorities.

The main prevention activities identified from a study of the company systems manual and discussions with a number of quality assurance department staff are matched against the model as follows.

A1   Quality engineering – planning.

The quality system and translating product design and customer quality requirements into manufacturing quality control of materials, processes and products. Implementing and maintaining quality plan and procedures.

This work is carried out exclusively within the quality assurance department. It absorbs most of the effort of two quality engineers. There is some input from the quality manager and from the quality engineering manager, and possibly from the quality assurance department foremen and inspectors.

A2   Design and development of quality measurement and control equipment.

This work falls wholly within the quality assurance department

A3   Quality planning by functions other than the quality assurance department.

This is an area where there may be significantly large inputs from other departments (e.g. purchasing, production engineering, manufacturing engineering and customer engineering) via such activities as the test house, gauge tables, planning inspection levels, and engineering concession authorizations.

A4   Calibration and maintenance of production equipment used to evaluate quality.

As defined this element does not match the situation at company 2. Such work as is done on this equipment is appraisal work (and hence in line with the ASQC categorization of this type of work).

A5   Maintenance and calibration of test and inspection equipment.

This work is carried out by calibration room staff and by external service laboratores. It should be noted that the ASQC categorizes this type of work under appraisal activities.

A6   Supplier assurance – the cost of personnel engaged in preventive activities of the supplier quality assurance programme.

This element is an important part of the preventive activities at company 2. It occupies a significantly large proportion of one quality assurance foreman's effort and there are inputs from purchasing, production engineering and metallurgical services on the site.

A7   Quality training.

The company is not active in providing outside training, but if it should become so, the costs should be easy to collect.

A8   Administration, audit, improvement and other costs.

Administration includes costs of secretarial services, telephones, travelling, etc. Audit costs are the costs of personnel engaged in planning, documenting, implementing and maintaining audits on the quality system. Improvement costs are the costs of the quality improvement process and motivational activities.

Administration costs are within the quality assurance department's control, and the audit and improvement activities are mostly from the audit inspector and the quality engineering manager respectively.

Comment

Activities of people within the quality assurance department which are substantial in terms of time consumed, which must have a preventive content, which are difficult to quantify and which may not be identified under the elements listed above are the daily review meetings, work aimed at changing from a corrective approach to a prevention-based/process control approach, involvement in reliability work, and post-warranty performance analysis. Similarly, the involvement of personnel from other functions (e.g. purchasing and production engineering) are difficult to quantify and cost.

However, overall, much of the activity is concentrated within the quality assurance department so that a good approximation of the prevention costs may be gained from estimates of man-hours spent on prevention activities and from the departmental budget.

If a cost breakdown under the different elements is desired, it is probably that estimates of time spent on the different activities would be so conflicting that one could have little confidence in them. This problem can only be overcome by requiring staff to keep records of how they spend their time. A weekly return accounting for activities in 10% (i.e. half-day) increments would be sufficient for the purpose. Secretarial and other costs could be allocated in direct proportion to the levels of the different activities, and outside services may be costed directly from invoices.

7.5.2 Appraisal costs

The definitions of appraisal costs used by BS and the ASQC are similar in intent despite differences in wording (e.g. BS's costs of assessing the quality achieved compared with the ASQC's costs incurred to determine the degree of conformance to quality requirements). With the exceptions noted earlier under prevention costs (A4, A5) the elements are almost identical. Some of the elements, however, clearly relate to large-scale heavy engineerng and are not applicable to the operations of company 2. The remaining categories cover appraisal activities reasonably well.

B1   Laboratory acceptance testing (of purchased materials).

This includes an input from production engineering which may be difficult to quantify, but costs of external testing should be easy to determine from invoices.

B2   Inspection and test (including goods inwards inspection).

This is probably the largest single cost element, including as it does the cost of all the inspection staff together with a substantial proportion of their supervisors' time, material review board time, and some management time.

B3   In-process inspection by personnel who are not inspectors by job description.

This may also be a fairly substantial cost, part of which may readily be measurable (e.g. production personnel engaged full time on testing) and some of which may be very difficult to measure (e.g. gauging by operators which may add to the time of the operation).

B4   Cost of setting up equipment or products for inspection or functional testing is largely covered in this case by B3 above (e.g. testing in service-like environment and subsequent stripping down for post-test inspection).

B5   Inspection and test materials include crack detection fluids, paper for machines, plaster of Paris, and losses of castings and shafts in testing. The items and sources of cost are very diverse and whilst some materials costs specific to quality or metallurgical functions may be relatively easy to collect from invoices, the costs incurred from production materials may be difficult to determine, not because material items costs are not known, but because the usages are not recorded.

B6   Product quality audits are a part-time activity of the audit inspector and could be costed from their time allocation data.

B7   Review of test and inspection data.

The practice of 100% inspection obviates the need for regular reviews of test and inspection data before release of the product for shipment.

B8   Field (on-site) performance testing.

Not applicable as defined.

B9   Internal testing and release.

Not appropriate as defined.

B10 Evaluation of field stock and spare parts.

Not appropriate as defined.

B11 Data processing inspection and test reports.

This activity occupies a significant fraction of the senior quality engineer's and the audit inspector's time, and there is a pro rata input from the quality manager.

Comment

Important appraisal cost elements not accounted for above are the depreciation cost of capital equipment used for inspection, gauging and balancing, and the costs of items needing frequent replacement. Presumably inventories and costs of all inspection and gauging equipment are available and should make these costs easily determinable.

7.5.3 Failure costs

Internal failure costs

There is good agreement between the BS and ASQC publications on the definition of internal failure costs (i.e. the costs arising within the manufacturing organization of the failure to achieve the quality specified – before transfer of ownership to the customer). There is also good agreement on the definitions of individual cost elements. The elements and their relevance to internal failure costs at company 2 are as follows.

C1   Scrap – all scrap losses incurred in the course of meeting quality requirements (scrap caused by overruns, obsolescence or design changes requested by customers are not included).

Although the points in the process at which parts are scrapped is noted on the process route traveller, no attempt is made to calculate the value at that point. The current practice is to cost scrap parts as material cost plus half the direct labour and overhead costs which would have been incurred if the item had been processed to completion. Periodic analysis of data from travellers and reject notes should demonstrate the aptness of the present practice, though some weighting should be applied to account for the segregation, marking and handling of scrap by indirect workers. A comparison between the numbers of replacement parts issued and the records of parts scrapped should indicate the amount of scrap which is not accounted for.

It is the practice in some companies to deduct the value of scrap parts from the scrap failure costs before presenting the quality cost statement. This, of course, is an understatement of failure costs and should be avoided.

C2   Rework and repair – the costs incurred in meeting quality requirements when material can be restored for use.

Rework is recorded but is not analysed and costed, though it is claimed that the decision to scrap or rework is taken on an economic basis. Clearly the distribution of rejected parts between scrap and rework should change with the economics of production at that time. The sensitivity of the economics under various conditions of production is not known in company 2.

In addition to the direct costs of rework there are costs for sorting and checking rejected batches and the costs of the involvement of production control and other personnel in replanning for rework. The cost of provision and use of equipment for carrying out rework, which cannot be accommodated on production line machines, should not be overlooked.

A complicating factor in the cost of rework is the practice of specifying the rework/excess work account when it is not possible to identify a particular department as being responsible for the machine time lost.

C3   Trouble shooting or defect/failure analysis.

There are inputs from the quality assurance department and the product engineering department.

C4   Reinspect, retest.

These activities are not noted directly but presumably could be estimated, if necessary, from knowledge of the amount and type of rework as a fraction of the total processing activity.

C5   Scrap and rework through fault of vendor.

Costs of material are recovered from the vendor but costs of processing material to the point of rework/scrap, and the costs of idle facilities and labour, are not recovered.

C6   Modification permits and concessions – the time spent reviewing product designs and specifications.

Because there are inputs from a number of people in many functions this cost may only be estimated. If the element is interpreted in the wider sense of the whole activity of obtaining qualifications, modification permits and concessions, together with the effects of delays, batch splitting, etc., the cost must be considerable and very difficult to quantify without detailed records of time inputs from all the staff involved.

C7   Downgrading.

This is usually taken to mean reclassification as 'seconds'. The company does not market 'seconds' though some components which are substandard for normal products may be able to be used satisfactorily in remanufactured units. Remanufacture or overhaul is not a quality-related cost and it is doubtful whether it is worthwhile considering the difference in value between standard components in normal production units and the downgraded components in the remanufactured units which are sold more cheaply.

Comment

Because scrap and rework costs are collected and probably amount to an impressive sum of money, there may be a tendency to assume it is the whole cost (or indeed a reluctance to investigate more closely in case it turns out to be even bigger). Nevertheless, the process economics used to decide whether to scrap or to reject are probably worth investigating because they may enable savings to be made. Similarly the booking of lost machine time to quality-related codes on spurious grounds may warrant investigation to make sure that the quality-related cost account is not being debited unfairly. In the matter of modification permits, etc., discussed under C6 above, it may be worthwhile doing a 'snapshot' costing to determine the magnitude, sources and causes of these costs. To attempt to collect them on a regular basis appears to be a horrendous task, even though the costs may be relatively large.

7.5.4 External failure costs

External failure costs are defined as the costs arising when products fail to meet quality requirements (after transfer of ownership to the customer). This is not an entirely satisfactory definition because it implies that all costs, irrespective of who incurs them, should be included. The BS definition, though slightly differently worded, has similar implications. Such costs may be of value to students of life cycle costing and reliability studies, but in this case the costs to be considered will be those quality-related costs incurred by the company.

D1   Complaints administration.

Complaints reach the company via several routes, e.g. customer service, marketing, production engineering, etc. Unless complaints are formally channelled through rigorous procedures and dealt with by a small number of people, it is difficult to see how such costs could be collected separately.

D2   Product or customer service, product liability (i.e. the costs of product services directly attributable to correcting imperfections, including any liability costs).

Costs incurred through the customer service organization of the company for products which, for example, fail on test or cause problems with fitting (as distinct from failure in service) could be collected under this heading. Isolating this element of expenditure would require a great deal of cooperation from customer service and other departments outside the control of the quality manager. In these circumstances, a decision about whether or not to gather these costs depends largely on the relative magnitude of the costs.

On the matter of product liability, the cost is probably carried by the vehicle manufacturer. If not, the costs incurred (which should be easily retrievable) or the requisite insurance premium costs should be included under this heading.

D3   Products rejected and returned, recalls, retrofits, the cost of handling and accounting for rejected products including any recall and retrofit costs.

It is unlikely that the handling and accompanying costs of this limited activity are sufficiently large to warrant them being identified separately.

D4   Returned material repair – the costs associated with analysing and repairing customer-returned material.

Such costs should be readily identifiable because of their non-routine nature and because of customer (i.e. external) involvement. Recovered material or components should not be credited to this account.

D5   Warranty replacement – the cost of replacing failures within the warranty period.

This cost should relate strictly to the replacement cost of the faulty item. Other costs incurred (e.g. investigation of warranty claims) should be included under D1 above.

The BS and ASQC documents suggest that these costs may be subdivided to show the warranty costs incurred from errors arising in different departments, e.g. marketing, engineering, production and quality assurance. Analysis of warranty claims may reveal sources of error but it is debatable whether quantifying blame by allocating costs is helpful in eliminating errors, or is worth the effort.

The value of material or components recovered from failed products should not be credited to the warranty account.

Comment

This category probably incurs the same type of problem that arises with internal failure cost, i.e. because a substantial cost is already known, there is little incentive to refine it further. Refining the costs may be difficult because the activity at the company–customer interface is not within the sphere of direct influence of the quality manager and hence would require an extremely high level of commitment and cooperation from the customer service and marketing functions. The costs involved may not warrant the effort, especially if there is little potential to reduce them.

7.6 Discussion of findings

In assessing the applicability of BS 6143 it appeared that the costs of most of the elements which are applicable could be ascertained without too much trouble, and it was surprising to learn that only five element costs were available directly from the accounts department without having to analyse cost data. This suggests a weakness in the matching of quality elements, as defined in BS 6143, with the kinds of cost data usually available in companies.

The difficulties of whether activities should be classified as being quality related, which arose at company 1, also arose at company 2. Examples here are provision of 'clean areas' and 'protection' for components and assemblies. Clearly cleanliness from abrasive dirt is important in the manufacture of high-speed delicately balanced machinery, but is the cost of ensuring it a quality-related cost? Other examples are the segregation, marking and handling of scrap, movement of goods for inspection purposes, the activities of purchasing and accounting personnel in dealing with rejected supplies, and the effects of order-splitting (for quality reasons) on planning and manufacture. From a quality viewpoint it may appear that these activities are quality related and should feature in quality-related costs. However, an accountant might argue that they should be omitted on grounds of difficulty of quantification alone.

Activities which are clearly quality related are those concerned with products passed on concession, and modifications. The feeling gained at company 1 that these are large, costly, but unmeasured activities was reinforced at company 2, perhaps because, although it is sensibly autonomous in its production operations, qualifications or changes to specification must be approved by the parent company in the United States, so that relatively minor matters can become quite protracted.

A quality cost which company 2 has no difficulty in defining (if only because it has been decisive about it) is the valuation of scrapped goods. Many quality management practitioners and accountants have some difficulty with this and opinions on the matter range from purchased materials costs to full selling price. Company 2 takes the view that it should be the full materials cost plus half the combined direct labour and overhead cost. Although the point in the process at which the item is scrapped is noted on the manufacturing route card, the company does not feel it is worth calculating the labour and overhead costs at every stage in the manufacturing process, and has settled on half of what these costs would have been if the item had been processed to completion. Because of company 2's relatively high materials costs, there seems little point in trying to refine it further.

Other minor points on costing worth noting from the work at company 2 are:

1. although scrap valuation includes overheads, rework costs do not;
2. apparently US tax law encourages companies to value all scrap at full sales value;
3. although there was good agreement between the accounts department and quality assurance department on scrap costs, there was no evidence of an independent check from a materials balance.

A noticeable feature of the accounting system at company 2 and that at other companies is the greater accountability the nearer one gets to the manufacturing operation. This has implications for the cost collection exercise because the bulk of quality costs are incurred close to the maufacturing operation. Hence the accountability bias is in the quality cost collector's favour. A factor working in the opposite direction is the involvement of personnel from a wide spectrum of functions. It is not usual for personnel in functions such as purchasing and accounting to make returns of how they spend their time. Indeed, it is the general lack of information about how people, other than direct workers, spend their time which presents a considerable obstacle to the collection of quality costs.

A pitfall waiting for the unwary was the reporting of changes in provision (e.g. for warranty) as opposed to actual expenditure in the period. According to the Institute of Cost and Management Accountants' [3] official terminology, provisions for liabilities and charges are:

> Amounts retained as reasonably necessary for the purpose of providing for any liability or loss which is either likely to be incurred, or certain to be incurred but uncertain as to amount or as to the date on which it will rise (Companies Acts).

Although this seems perfectly straightforward, problems can arise for cost collectors because the provision for a particular liability may be topped up with arbitrary amounts of money from time to time. Hence to determine the true expenditure it is necessary to know about the topping up as well as the change in provision. A more familiar trap met with was the reporting of net costs of scrap. The errors which may be unwittingly introduced by this practice are quite large in company 2's case, because many of its components are made of expensive alloys which have a high scrap value.

The use of costs as motivators to shopfloor workers in company 2 was interesting. The costs displayed were the costs of scrapped goods, because shopfloor workers could see the relevance of them to their work. Further, although the scrap costs are relatively small in company cost terms, they are large in relation to the wages of operatives on the factory shopfloor. Thus a strong impact is made without disclosing sensitive cost information.

Table 7.1 Quality-related cost report – company 2

	£000	%	Total (%)	Annual sales turnover (%)
Prevention				
Laboratory and other services	23	21		
Quality engineering	38	35		
Calibration room	26	24		
Supplier quality assurance	12	11		
Administration and other costs	10	9		
	109	100	6.6	0.38
Appraisal				
Quality control	430	61		
Test	200	28		
Product inspection	6	1		
Gauges	32	5		
Operating supplies*	12	2		
Laboratory services	7	1		
Quality audit	12	2		
	699	100	42.3	2.4
Internal failure				
Scrap*	276	52.5		
Rework*	135	25.8		
Materials Review Board (production)	45	8.7		
Materials Review Board (quality)	12	2.3		
Data processing	4	0.7		
Purchasing/manufacturing engineering/product engineering	53	10.0		
	525	100	31.8	1.8
External failure				
Warranty*	37	11.6		
Abnormal warranty*	116	36.4		
Rejected materials*	16	5.0		
Service/administration/other	150	47.0		
Total	319	100	19.3	1.1
Overall total	1652		100.0	6.1

*Total figures obtainable from accounts department. Other figures estimated.

7.7 Cost report and comparison with other data

At the time of the study, by pure coincidence, there was a company-wide initiative in collecting quality costs taking place and the quality manager was preparing a quality cost report. The quality-related costs collected are listed by element and category in Table 7.1. They amount to £1.65 million, equivalent to 6.1% of the annual sales turnover in the year the study was conducted. The distribution between categories is broadly as expected and, also, within categories there are a few elements which account for a large proportion of the cost.

When a first cost report is complete it is natural to wonder whether the performance it reflects is good, bad or indifferent. In a company like this, with a number of competing manufacturing divisions, it should be possible to make inter-divisional comparisons of quality performance using numbers of rejects, etc., as well as costs. This internal comparison is one of the methods employed in competitive benchmarking. Unfortunately, the company has not yet developed its quality-related costing systems to such a state that meaningful comparisons may be made. Indeed it is doubtful whether even the reporting of numbers is uniform enough for valid comparisons to be made. An alternative is to wait until another report is completed, perhaps a year later, and look for differences. Again, unfortunately, this would not give an absolute measure of performance. Hence a comparison has been made with published data despite the dangers of doing so which have been stressed on numerous occasions in this book.

The data used are those from a survey carried out by the journal *Quality* [4] in which are reported categories of quality costs as percentages of total quality costs and of net sales billed NSB (turnover) for several industry groups at two levels of sophistication of cost collection (Table 7.2).

Keeping in mind the limitations of the data, it appears that company 2 is more akin to companies with a formal programme for cost collection and engaged in the manufacture of instruments, etc., than to any other group. Gross expenditure as a percentage of annual sales turnover is similar to other manufacturers but the prevention expenditure appears to be low in both absolute terms and as a proportion of quality-related expenditures. Appraisal costs are high, which is consistent with low external failure and slightly high internal failure costs.

7.8 Presentation and uses of cost data

It was interesting to note the difference in the formats devised by the quality manager at company 2 and the proposed format from elsewhere

Table 7.2 Company 2: quality-related costs compared with some industry sector costs

Comparison of company 2 performance with published data*	Formal programme for cost collection								Informal programme for cost collection		
	Total % Net sales billed	Prev. % NSB	Appr. % NSB	Int. Fail. % NSB	Ext. Fail. % NSB	Scrap (S) % NSB	Rework (R) % NSB	Warranty (W)† % NSB			
Company 2	6.1	0.38	2.4	1.8	1.1	0.95	0.47	0.52			
Machinery manufacture	4.43	0.49	1.05	1.76	1.14	2.5	1.5	2.2			
Instruments, etc. manufacture	7.27	1.20	2.12	1.78	2.15	3.6	2.8	1.8			
Manufacturing industry in general	5.8	0.6	1.5	2.5	1.2	3.2	3.0	1.6			
	Total Q. cost	Prev. %	Appr. %	Int. Fail. %	Ext. Fail. %	Scrap % S+R+W	Rework % S+R+W	Warranty† % S+R+W			
Company 2	100	6.6	42.3	31.8	19.3	49	24	27			
Machinery manufacture	100	11	24	40	26	40	25	35			
Instruments, etc. manufacture	100	16.5	29	24.5	29.5	44	34	22			
Manufacturing industry in general	100	10.3	26	43	20.7	41	38	21			

*Quality costs survey. Quality, June 1977, pp. 20–2 [4].
†Warranty includes abnormal warranty.

in the company. The former reflects the day-to-day quality-related activities as the quality manager experiences them whilst the proposed format is a copy of the received wisdom on the subject, modified to suit the company's *modus operandi* rather than its needs (whatever these may be). It is interesting too to note that the quality manager's original listing of quality-related cost elements was not categorized under prevention/appraisal/failure headings. That came later, presumably, to fit in with the received wisdom. The point is important because the original intent was simply to establish a list of cost elements and an agreed method of calculation of costs so that valid inter-site comparisons could be made. Categorization of these elements into prevention/appraisal/failure costs adds nothing to the usefulness or value of the data for their intended purpose. Nor is the proposed format accompanied by any justification for that particular format. It does not appear to help the company in what it is attempting to achieve and indeed one of the dangers of picking up ready-made formats is that important elements may get left out simply because they do not fit conveniently into one of the prescribed pigeon-holes. While predetermined formats and checklists may have much to commend them in helping less knowledgeable people to compile reports, there is no substitute for experience. Nor does this form of reporting help to identify directly projects for quality improvement, though the subsidiary scrap numbers and cost report is useful for this purpose.

References

1. BS 6143 (1981) *The Determination and Use of Quality-Related Costs*, British Standards Institution, London.
2. ASQC Quality Costs Committee (1974) *Quality Costs – What and How*, American Society for Quality Control, Milwaukee, WI.
3. Anon (1982) *Management Accounting: Official Terminology of the ICMA*, Institute of Cost and Management Accountants, London.
4. Anon (1977) Quality cost survey. *Quality*, 20–2.

8

Case study, company 3

8.1 Introduction

Company 3 is engaged in the manufacture of diesel engines for powering trucks, buses, trains and pumping stations. The type of production is medium-scale batch machining and fabrication, assembly and test. It employs 1300 people and has a sales turnover of about £48 million per annum.

Although it is a subsidiary part of one of a large group of companies it is an autonomous business unit set up in 1981 with all the usual functional departments except engineering and sales, which are centralized functions of the parent company. Sister units within the parent company are important suppliers and customers of company 3, and a sister company to the parent company is also a major customer.

Since becoming 'independent', company 3 has achieved remarkable changes in its quality performance. In a little over three years it has, for example, reduced its inspection staff by two-thirds and reduced defects per engine, detected at audits, from 30 to three. However, there has been little corresponding evidence of cost improvement. Thus the development of cost measurement and reporting was lagging behind the improvements in product and service quality. It should also be mentioned that the company's products often do not go into service immediately after manufacture, and when in service they remain operational for a relatively long time (typically three to ten years). Hence it takes a long time (perhaps one to three years) for the effects of quality improvement, as measured at the factory, to be noticed in the marketplace. The improvements have been achieved in a climate of very difficult trading circumstances for their major in-house customers and the company is always actively seeking new customers and applications for its engines.

Inevitably the quality management objectives, strategies, behaviour and attitudes within the parent company will have their influence on daughter companies. The situation of the parent company with respect to quality costs is that they have, in the past, monitored costs but not used them. At the time the work was being conducted they were attempting to collate quality cost reports from the seven daughter companies. It was interesting to note that the headquarters quality function was trying to collate costs listed by activity from seven different operations under the usual prevention–appraisal–failure categories, as laid down in their quality policy manual. This was despite the fact that the policy manual is itself subdivided into functional activities and the only reference to categorization of activities under prevention–appraisal–failure is in the policy on costs.

The focus of the work reported and discussed in this chapter was to identify and analyse the available quality cost information and examine how it might be used.

8.2 Identification of sources of quality costs

In this case study the approach adopted to the identification of quality-related costs was initially that used in company 2, i.e. the company's operating procedures and costing systems were scrutinized to identify items which might refer to quality-related activities or costs. In addition, there was much information to be gleaned from monthly reports on quality-related activities. This was most notably in the fields of suppliers, in-house failures and warranty. The parent company quality policy manual also gave clues to where quality-related costs might be found. A paper on quality-related costs from a similar industry (Schmidt and Jackson [1]) added nothing to this part of the exercise. It merely served to endorse the information found in company 3's documents and records.

8.3 Cost sources identified from procedures and systems

The company's operating procedures are grouped under seven categories:

1. procedure information
2. finance
3. quality
4. production
5. manufacturing engineering

6. personnel
7. materials department

All the procedures were examined for leads to quality-related costs. The company's accounting systems and reports were also scrutinized with the same objective. Both of these searches were supplemented by discussion with company staff as appropriate. In the event this part of the exercise was not so fruitful as expected and much more was gained from studying quality cost reporting as practised in the company.

The principal points noted from this part of the exercise are offered without comment as potential pointers to other quality cost collectors as follows.

- Instructions for booking direct labour hours, including excess hours (some of which are due to quality-related matters), are described under financial procedures.
- Some machine shop rectification work is done by setters and by apprentices.
- Measured excess time bookings are recorded on operation cards and authorized by the industrial engineering department.
- Performances and costings are derived from the data on operation cards.
- Of 15 excess time codes three are positively quality related (defective material, previous operation defective, rectifications), whilst others may be so (e.g. equipment defective or temporary, alternative material or method, fitting shortages) depending on the underlying reasons and the view of what is or what is not a quality-related activity.
- Labour-booking procedures for additional unplanned operations raise many questions about what is or what is not quality-related work even though only four of 12 categories are the responsibility of the quality assurance department and become the subject of a standard quality non-conformance report.
- Labour performance reporting is by weekly tabulation of analyses of booked hours. Among the many analyses carried out are excess and indirect bookings by direct workers, measured and unmeasured excess hours by type, part number, operation number and operator.
- Four of eight quality non-conformance liability codes are related to suppliers and customers.
- Procedures specify that 'agreed costs' for sorting, fitting, etc. should be recovered by the purchasing department from suppliers of defective parts.
- Manufacturing engineering supply estimates of additional costs are incurred owing to defective material from suppliers.

- In-plant rectification costs of defects which are the supplier's liability are negotiated with the supplier prior to the work being done.
- Matters which are, or are likely to be, passed on concession do not become the subject of quality non-conformance reports.
- Procedures for production concessions and engineering design modifications make no reference to cost allocation of the activities involved.
- If rectification is not possible, the foreman will determine, in conjunction with inspection, if a concessionary procedure can be involved. This indicates that the concession is a second resort for the disposal of non-confirming parts and products.
- When non-conforming parts are the result of careless workmanship, the operator concerned is expected to rectify them without a time allowance being given. When the operator responsible cannot rectify the work for some reason, someone else does it and is recompensed for it.
- Rectification costs incurred on bought-out materials are net of recharge to suppliers.
- The quality assurance department analyses quality non-conformance rejects weekly and collates defect incidence against cost to produce a 'top-ten' machine shop scrap report.
- The finance department receives scrap analysis data from the quality assurance department as well as quality non-conformance reports to assist with the compilation of scrap costs analysed by manufacturing area.
- Scrap valuation for quality cost purposes is direct materials cost and direct labour (at base hourly rate) to the point of scrapping. For stock valuation purposes an overhead on direct labour is included.
- Parts downgraded for service use may incur unplanned additional work which is not picked up as a quality cost.
- Finished parts found to be non-conforming after being passed to stores, assembly or goods inward are not the subject of a quality non-conformance report but costs of rectification are picked up by use of appropriate accounting codes on the operations card.
- Rectification costs are gathered under headings of bought-out material, made-in components, and rectification of incomplete assembly work. They are collected across the site and are not analysed by department.
- Modification work costs are also gathered on a site basis against modifications to rejected products and modification of components to new specifications.
- Quality circle costs are identified separately but quality training costs are not.

- The whole engine test operation is regarded as a quality cost and is under the control of the quality assurance manager.
- The purchasing department performance reports made no reference to their supplier quality assurance activities and related improvements.

8.4 Quality cost collection and analysis

8.4.1 General

At company 3 an outstanding feature was the infectious enthusiasm of the quality assurance manager in leading a crusade for continuous and never-ending quality improvement. His views of what constituted quality cost, and in particular failure costs, were challenging, stimulating and enlightening. His philosophy focuses attention of management failures as well as shopfloor failures. Guilty managers could run but they could not escape from the logic of the cases against them.

The parent company's policy on quality costs and improvements states that the quality cost report must show prevention, appraisal and failure categories. Company 3's procedures and accounting practices do not make any such specification. Nor are they set up to produce quality-related costs in that format on a routine basis.

In addition to the policy statement a curious memorandum which originated within the parent company describes the concept of total quality costs as follows:

Total Quality Cost is designed to identify all the costs of not getting the product right first time. It therefore includes the following major costs broken down into different categories where appropriate:

* the cost of employing the total quality function (hourly paid wages, salaries and all related benefits)
* the cost of all production workers' time booked to remedying quality defects (rectification, etc.)
* all obsolete stock provisions
* the costs of implementing engineering design modifications on current models
* all bookings to scrap (labour and materials)
* estimates for new model testing work
* warranty expenditure for the period (not the charge to the profit and loss account which would include the movement in warranty provision in addition, but the actual expenditure).

On the matter of measurement the memorandum goes on:

From the above categories it can be seen that the collection of relevant cost data needs to be done by recognising that all costs booked to certain cost centres or account codes are considered as quality costs, and are collected as such . . .

The other way to approach the costing would be in terms of heads employed on quality which could then be adjusted by the appropriate wage or salary rate to give the cost of employing those heads. Additional adjustments could then be made for scrap costs, obsolete stock provision, warranty costs and product design costs . . .

Obviously the first approach will give more accurate numbers if the costs are recorded in this detail. The second approach should give a method of producing a fairly accurate estimate of total quality cost if the cost centre/account code detail is not available. Either will represent a significant improvement over current practice.

The inclusion of obsolete stock provision is unusual on two counts because (1) a provision is not an expenditure and (2) (in company 3 at least) obsolete stock is defined as material for which there is no forward requirement. The inclusion of new model testing work as a quality-related cost is also unusual. Most people would regard these costs as development costs. However, the points about the implementation of engineering design modifications and reporting of warranty expenditure are well made.

Notwithstanding the policies and guidelines of the parent company, company 3 reports quality costs on a routine basis in ways which suit its own business, technology and processes. Hence its first-level expression of quality costs is through the scrap costs of its in-house machining operations in order to identify which of several quality problems to tackle. Monthly quality performance reports, using a presentation format similar to that used for cost control versus budget, show an array of appraisal and failure data together with a limited amount of cost data for each of 23 machining areas operating under separate cost centres. Part of the cost data is the cost of scrap, also expressed as cost per effective standard hour (ESH). (An effective standard hour is a standard hour's output of piece parts, assemblies or process operations, excluding all excesses, which are directly attributable to a finished product. The standard per piece multiplied by the quantity gives the total ESH produced.) The cost of rework and the inspection costs associated with it (including sorting) are also reported.

Data from these records for the year in which the study was carried out have been used to compile the histograms shown in Figure 8.1 to illustrate the change in perspective of problems which is brought about by presenting failure rate data on a cost basis instead of the usual number-of-failures basis. The effect is dramatic and is by no means uncommon. The implications of the change in perspective may also be dramatic because solutions to the major problems, as defined using

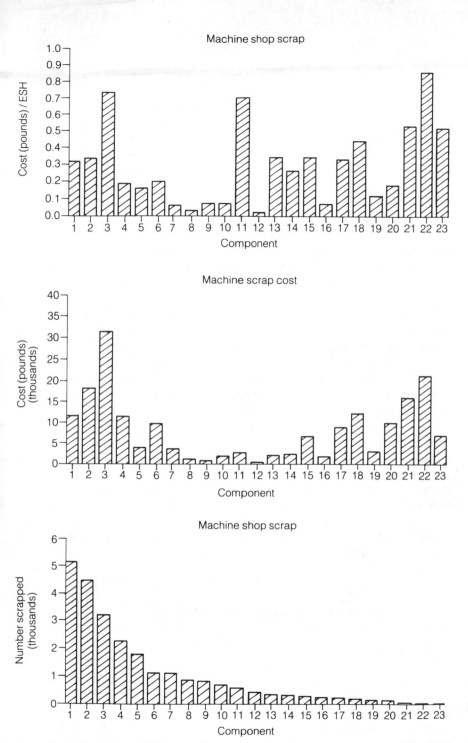

Figure 8.1 Scrap Costs of in-house manufacturing operations.

the different bases, may call for very different amounts and kinds of resources.

The same kind of exercise cannot be done for rework (using the data as presented) because only cost, and not number, data for rework are presented in the report, though the numerical data must surely be known. However, if it is accepted that cost is the proper criterion against which to gauge the importance of problems, then the rework and associated cost data may also be used to identify problems warranting the allocation of high-priority limited resources. Figure 8.2 indicates the relative importance of problem areas using scrap value versus rework and associated costs, though it must be borne in mind that the magnitude of scrap costs are generally much greater than rework and associated costs. The changes in distribution which occur when translating scrap levels from numbers to costs, and then to costs per effective standard hour, are very marked. Such drastic changes are not uncommon, and whilst they may give immediate indications of which problems should be being tackled, it is worth noting that different ways of expressing the cost produce different indications. Hence it is important to try to determine and use the cost expression which is right for a company at that time, also keeping in mind that different problems may require quite different resources and have widely different timescales for solutions to be devised and implemented.

The prevention, appraisal and production testing activities of company 3 are executed under cost centres under the control of the quality assurance manager and the costs are reported routinely for budgetary control purposes. These costs together with the in-house failure costs discussed above comprise the majority of the in-house quality costs featured in the company's monthly quality cost reports. However, just as internal failure costs are the subject of close scrutiny and analysis to identify and rank problem areas, so, also, are the failure aspects of the company's external dealings with suppliers and customers given special attention.

8.4.2 Suppliers of rough and finished goods
The quality performance of suppliers of bought-out finished goods is closely monitored. All goods go through the goods receiving section of stores. Some goods which pass goods inward inspection may be rejected from the production line. Rejections from either source are coded to indicate the reason for the rejection and the fact that it is the supplier's responsibility. Sometimes with certain suppliers the company is able to recover from the supplier a nominal sum to cover associated costs such as removal of the component/unit, obtaining a replacement from stores, refitting and retesting. Costs to be recovered for sorting or

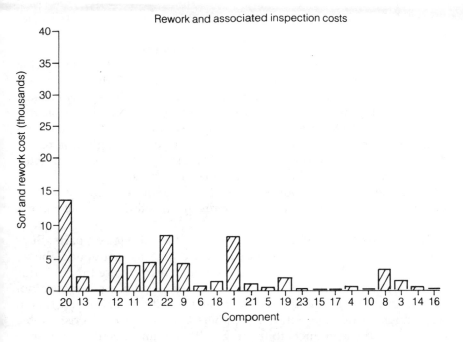

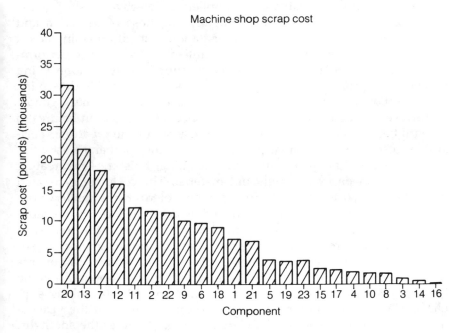

Figure 8.2 Rework, inspection and scrap cost analysis.

correcting non-conforming goods are usually agreed with the supplier before the work is done.

Some finished materials failures do not show up until after they have been fitted to engines or at engine test. All defects detected during engine build and test are noted in the so-called 'Black Museum' report (including failures of parts made in-house). A very serious view is taken of items in this report because, clearly, the costs of correction at this late stage of manufacture can be very high, to say nothing of the effects on the production schedule and productivity. Interestingly this report does not deal in proportions or percentages; it reports absolute numbers on the grounds that the ultimate objective must be zero defects. Although the data are reported formally only monthly, the situation is monitored continuously and formal review meetings are held every week.

Requisitions are raised for the replacement of all rejected parts. Suppliers are charged for faulty goods supplied and, as mentioned above, in some cases additional associated costs may be recovered though this is unlikely to happen with in-house suppliers. The company does not have a simple inspect and reject relationship with its suppliers. It is in continuous negotiation with its suppliers and gives them considerable feedback on their products to try to get them to improve their performance.

Much of the cost associated with suppliers of defective finished goods is recoverable. The costs to the company are those of detection and handling of the goods and the administration costs of obtaining credit or replacements. These costs are not identified separately. The performance data are used to rank and classify suppliers. It is done using numbers and proportions of rejects, not costs, and is used to determine the inspection level and frequency to be applied to the suppliers' goods.

However, cost data are an important aspect of the data on failures to do with bought-out rough material. The reason for the greater importance of costs here is that a large proportion of the company's activities (and hence costs) are taken up with machining, finishing and treating components made from bought-out material. The costs are generated from standard costs and from information noted on the quality non-conformance report. They are produced as a monthly computer tabulation and are abstracted and featured as part of a monthly report in which suppliers are ranked by percentages of components scrapped, by scrap value, and by labour costs incurred in machining components subsequently scrapped due to faults ascribable to the supplier. It is the labour costs incurred which is the principal criterion in ranking suppliers. The data are presented for the current month and the year-to-date so that persistently poor performers are kept under the spotlight. The analysis is carried further to show, for each of the top-ten worst suppliers, a ranking of components (e.g. cylinder liner, cylinder head, crankcase) by number and percentage scrapped and the wasted labour costs incurred. Hence the company has a very clear picture of what problems it should be taking up, and with which suppliers. Equally importantly, the costs, which include overheads on direct labour, are also expressed in the report as costs per effective standard hour, thus making them comparable with other costs incurred by the company.

It is interesting to speculate whether companies take into account the different amounts and types of quality resources in bought-out finished material and bought-out rough material when pondering the make or buy decision.

It is also noteworthy that despite some good work on vendor development the purchasing department does not feature this topic in its monthly purchasing performance report.

8.4.3 Warranty and service reports

At the other end of the operation warranty costs and field service problems similarly receive close attention. Warranty cover is divided into four categories: (1) 'zero-month warranty' (i.e. defects discovered and corrected between delivery to the vehicle builder and delivery to the customer); (2) 'campaign warranty' which covers authorized campaigns to have specific known faults corrected free of charge even though they may not have caused problems on a particular vehicle; (3) 'in warranty' which is normal warranty work correcting failures which have occurred whilst the vehicle has been in service within the warranty period or mileage; and (4) 'out of warranty' which covers very exceptional situations where an engine has been in service for longer than 12 months, or in excess of 100 000 miles, but the company may still give warranty cover.

When a problem in the field is identified as recurring sufficiently often to warrant an investigation, a service problem report is prepared to initiate the investigation in either company 3 or in the engineering department of the parent company, depending on the problem. The criterion for deciding where to deal with the problem initially is whether the solution calls for an engineering design modification to be made. If not it goes to company 3, though their findings may well result in it going back to the engineering department. From these systems the company acquires a considerable amount of quality and reliability data to assist with planning its design and manufacturing quality assurance activities.

On the matter of quality costs, warranty claims from customers are settled by the vehicle builder who then attempts to recover, from company 3, costs relating to engines. As mentioned earlier, most of the company's products go into vehicles built by the parent company and fall into two groups. The feedback from the first of the groups contains a lot of detail about how costs are built up. Computer tabulations display costs of labour and materials, other charges (e.g. towing), handling/administration charges (10% of materials cost), and landing charges (import duties, etc.), together with details of the defect, engine, vehicle, customer, dealer, etc. At one time there was a startlingly high incidence of false warranty claims arising from mistakes, deviousness, attempted deception and downright dishonesty. The automatic payment-without-question policy for settling small bills had contributed to this. The quality assurance department staff at company 3 check the tabulations and separate out all claims over £400 and claims which look 'suspicious' because of wrong coding of defects, vehicle type, etc. For example, in one month the company had 700 claims from this source. After examining the claims 197 of them were resisted. This scrutiny of claims is reckoned to be saving the company 3 12–15% of claimed warranty charges. This indicates that the effort of analysing and scrutinizing claims has been handsomely rewarded and will be especially so in other large companies having automatic payment systems. Among the other data derived from the tabulations are defects per engine and corresponding costs per engine versus time.

Data from the second outlet are not in the same form. These are data which have been processed by the quality assurance and reliability functions of the parent company. They are in the form of a warranty and service problem history of each vehicle from the day it is built to the expiry of warranty. Although these data also contain cost information it is not so readily retrievable as from the first set of data, though of course simple records of warranty payments without data about defects, etc. can be obtained from normal accounting records.

In the course of looking at warranty costs and discussions with the quality assurance department staff responsible for analysing the data a number of interesting points were raised.

- Warranty costs can be the sins of the father being visited upon the sons. In one case an engine went into service four years after being built. It failed in service and was rectified in the same year. The claim was not submitted until two years later.
- Some distributors have high incidences of particular problems which other distributors do not experience with the same engine type.
- Some individual vehicles are the subject of many small claims – usually for non-returnable parts.
- Some distributors' claims are frequently for sums just below the automatic payment-without-question limit.
- Analysis of the top 100 defects, as defined by claims (listing the top 100 faults corresponds to reviewing incidence of defects down to a

level of 0.3 defects per 100 vehicles) on a set of 216 vehicles showed a different content and pattern from a similar analysis on a set of 868 vehicles of a different type, but having the same engine.

- Successful auditing of warranty claims requires a thorough working knowledge of the manufacturing and testing process, history and development, as well as the uses of the product. A knowledge of commercial practices and a suspicious mind are also valuable assets.

The third aspect of post-manufacture external failure costs is that of service problem reports. The immediate problem as it affects the customer will of course be taken care of under the warranty scheme but with frequently recurring or chronic problems raising a service problem report initiates further in-house work and costs. When the problem is dealt with by quality assurance and manufacturing people it usually involves a tightening up of procedures and practices and the cost is lost in the overhead, of which quality assurance and manufacturing engineering and supervision are a part. Problems directed to the engineering function (which is a headquarters department of the parent company) usually result in the production of an engineering design modification. Again, the cost is not measured. But it raises the whole question of costs arising from engineering design modification and engineering concessions.

8.4.4 Engineering design modifications and concessions

Design modifications may be initiated by better design techniques, the opportuniy or need to change materials used in the product's construction, better machining capability, persistent field failures, etc. There are company procedures for controlling the modifications and rigorous systems for progressing requests for modifications through to acceptance and establishment. It is not the intention here to give details of the system but rather to give an indication of the size and character of the activity.

For example, the company's imprest system permits expenditure of up to £10 000 per month and up to £5 000 on any single design modification proposal. Furthermore, the time taken to process modifications from proposal to acceptance indicates the depth of involvement, whilst the facts of there being around 100 proposed modifications under consideration at any one time and 400 per year implemented show it to be a sizeable activity.

Concession to use components which do not meet specification may be sought for many reasons. Among them are the following.

- Materials already purchased and put into stock may be found not to conform to the purchasing specification.

- The vehicle assembly plant may be unable to build to specification and may seek to use alternative parts.
- Material shortages may force the company to switch to a new supplier at short notice.
- Components may be close but not exactly to specification.

Various uses of concession systems include overriding inspectors' decisions to reject components, seeking the engineering department's advice on matters not covered by specifications, and using concessions to bypass systems guarding against the too-ready introduction of modifications.

Disadvantages of concession systems are that their use sometimes induces lax attitudes towards quality such that the number of parts or the concession time period may be overrun in the knowledge that the concession can be renewed, and there may be a lack of urgency in tackling the cause of a problem for the same reason. Concession systems also proliferate paperwork since the subsequent disposal of every part of assembly should be the subject of a permanent record. Items which are passed on concession are really non-conforming items and the activities they generate are clearly quality related, as are many of those to do with design modifications, though neither is costed. Data have already been quoted to indicate the level of activity in design modifications. Add to these the fact that 9% of engines are passed on concession and one is left in no doubt that there is a sizeable quality activity slipping through the quality costing net. A contributory factor to failure to pick up modification and concession costs is that they are the subject of a quality non-conformance report, which is the principal documentation for picking up failure costs.

8.5 Quality cost reporting

Details of the reporting and use of costs of scrap have been discussed in the preceding section. However, in addition to these reports the quality assurance department and accounts department produce a quality cost report as part of the company's monthly operating review. All the costs which are used are taken from the company's standard accounting data. An example of the report as it finally appears is shown in Figure 8.3.

The way in which the costs are built up is illustrated in Figure 8.4. Down the left-hand side of this figure are the accounting sources from which the costs are abstracted. The majority of them are cost centres using budgetary control, some are derived from labour-bookings to quality-related codes and the remainder derive from invoices, stock records and quality non-conformance reports. Because the accounting

	Period 12		Full Year	
	Actual	% Sales revenue	Actual	% Sales revenue
Prevention costs				
Quality planning	£29788	1.0	£277833	0.6
Quality audit	4080	0.1	49926	0.1
Maintenance and calibration	911	—	15365	-
Total prevention costs	£34779	1.1	£343124	0.7
Appraisal costs				
Vendor inspection	£6218	0.2	£71859	0.1
In-process and final inspection	34211	1.1	424719	0.9
Engine test	57495	1.9	619135	1.3
Total appraisal costs	£97924	3.2	£1115713	2.3
Failure costs				
Design change	£35000	1.2	£420000	0.9
Rework	15732	0.5	253277	0.5
Scrap	(48775)	(1.6)	291225	0.6
Warranty	197000	6.5	2215000	4.6
Total failure costs	£198957	6.6	£3179502	6.6
Total quality costs	£331660	10.9	£4638339	9.6
Sales revenue base	£30080000		£48233000	

Figure 8.3 Quality cost summary.

system was not set up with the preparation of quality cost reporting in mind there are inherent problems in its use for that purpose. The limitations of the available data and their appropriateness for such a report are worthy of some discussion.

Quality assurance department staff salaries is a large sum which would probably justify being broken down into quality activities. Whilst the activities of the quality assurance manager, engineers and technicians are mainly prevention oriented, they do not spend all their time planning for quality. For example, one technician is engaged full time on vendor-related activities and another on warranty matters. Nor does this section admit contributions to quality planning (or any other prevention activity other than quality circles) by persons outside the quality assurance department.

Item	Cost centre Expense code	Quality cost element	Prevention Vendor planning	Quality planning	Dual audit	Maint'ce & calibr'n	Appraisal Vendor insp'n	Process & final test	Engine change	Internal failure Design	Rework	Scrap	External failure Warranty
1	1630	Quality department staff costs		202644									
2	1634	Heat treatment – salaried staff		34400									
3	1630	Quality department materials, services, etc.		40320									
4	L5520	Quality circles			49926								
5	1631	Audit inspection		469									
6	–	Maintenance and calibration of quality fixtures				15365							
7	1635	Goods receiving inspection					62268						
8	I/L4301	Direct labour inspection					9591						
9	1632	Component machining inspection						130068					
10	1633	Component machining inspection						136969					
11	1636	Component machining and assembly inspection						16344					
12	1637	Engine assembly inspection						31357					
13	1638	Coppersmith's inspection						15684					
14	1639	Final inspections						59610					
15	–	Laboratory recharge						34687					
16	1683	Engine test – inspector's							37408				
17	1680	Engine test							263194				
18	1682	Pre- and post-test work							148069				
19	–	Engine test materials and purchased services							170464				
20	–	Obsolete stock								420000			
21	1681	Sick bay – Engine test									21919		
22	1866	Pre-test 'snagging'									159689		
23	–	Rectification and modifications (excl. item 22)									71669		
24	–	Scrap (materials and labour)										291225	
25	–	Warranty											2215000
		Total	–	277833	49926	15365	71859	424719	619135	420000	253277	291225	2215000
		% Quality-related cost		6	1.1	0.3	1.6	9.2	13.3	9	5.5	6.3	47.7
		% Quality-related cost		7.4			24.1				20.8			47.7
		% Sales revenue		0.7			2.3				2.0			4.6

Figure 8.4 Quality cost synthesis

Quality audits here mean audits on components and assemblies, not systems. These are presumably included in the staff salaries figure.

The costs gathered under the inspection headings are salary data abstracted from the budgets of each cost centre. Costs of inspection work by direct workers have overheads included. Inspection of their own work by operators is not costed. Nor are the involvements of production and engineering personnel in twice weekly scrap patrols, concession considerations, engine audits and other appraisal activities.

Engine test is an interesting inclusion. Some would argue that one cannot reasonably expect to build anything so complicated as an engine and not expect to have to make adjustments to it and run it before putting it into a vehicle; that this is all part of the manufacturing process; and that it is not a quality cost. However, the testing operation does much more than this. It is used to run-in engines, check pressures and flows, fuel consumption, exhaust-gas composition, etc. The whole operation, involving a host of complicated mechanical, electrical, hydraulic and computing equipment, is under the control of the quality assurance manager, which clearly indicates the company view that it is a quality-related activity. Costs noted are personnel salaries and materials usages only. Maintenance, servicing, occupation costs and depreciation on this very expensive asset are not included in the costs.

The item 'Obsolete stock' is a curious one. In discussion with the appropriate accounts manager it was learned that obsolete stock is defined as stock in hand, at the annual stock check, for which there is no forward requirement of the next 12 months. Overstocking may come about by panic buying, purchasing supposedly economic batch quantities, or by speculative orders. The stocks become surplus to requirements because of design changes, even though requests for engineering design modifications should take full account of existing stocks. Obsolete stock is not necessarily disposed of. The value of just-in-time purchasing becomes clear when situations such as this surface. The relationship between obsolete stock and quality-related costs is a tenuous one, unless one takes the view that (1) there is an implicit failure in being left with £420 000 worth of obsolete stock, and (2) all costs of systems failures are quality costs.

Costs of rectification of parts to new specifications derive from labour-bookings by direct workers, a data source not noted for its veracity or accuracy in most companies. To compound any inherent inaccuracy in the data the figures are inflated by a factor of five or more by the inclusion of overheads. It is noteworthy that in company 3 scrap costs are always kept under the spotlight and featured in so much reporting that there is a good chance they may be reasonably accurate.

Sources of cost data for the broad exercise of compiling the total quality costs are mostly cost centres or financial codes. There is little cost breakdown or cross-boundary analysis of the type which is usually necessary to trigger the uncovering of hidden costs. This, coupled with the known omissions noted above, probably means that the costs are underestimated by a considerable degree. The standard of reporting is poor. Reports do not separate out costs as an aspect of quality worthy of presentation and comment in its own right. This is a pity, because there is a lot of cost information available which is not being used to its full potential.

Overall the reporting probably understates the company's quality costs in those areas where the cost is reckoned only as salaries, but this may be counterbalanced by the inclusion of obsolete stocks and overheads on direct worker costs. However, if this is true, even the omission of costs of personnel from other departments involved in quality, of inputs from the parent company, and of quality ramifications of the concession and design modification systems means the report may understate the costs to a considerable degree.

A first inclination might be to vilify the accounts department for this. That would be unfair. Management accountants are usually willing to cooperate in collecting quality costs, but need guidance from quality people on what to measure.

8.6 Comparison of performance with other published data

The case which needs to be taken when making comparisons between sets of data from different sources has been strongly emphasized in Chapter 1 and has been reiterated in the earlier case studies. Nevertheless companies like to know how their performance compares with others. In this case, by good fortune, there are data published by a company in the same business. Also, of course, there are the US survey data [2] drawn upon in the other case studies. The temptation was too strong and the comparison was made, with the anomalous results now described which serve to reinforce the warnings about comparisons of quality cost data.

The data from the same industry are those of Schmidt and Jackson [1] from the Detroit Allison Division of General Motors in the United States. Although on a cursory reading they appear to claim that quality costs total 6.3% of sales revenue made up of 'prevention' 0.3%, 'remedial engineering' 1%, 'external appraisal' 1%, and 'internal appraisal' 4%, they provide data to enable their quality-related costs to be shown to amount to 11.8% of sales revenue made up as follows: prevention 0.3%, remedial engineering 0.9%, external appraisal 0.7%, internal appraisal 4%, warranty and policy 4%, scrap 1.8% and product liability 0.1%.

In attempting to compare the above data with those of company 3 and with the US survey data, there is an immediate problem with differences in terminology because Schmidt and Jackson do not use the conventional categorization of quality costs. Hence, if a comparison is to be made, some interpretations of the terminology must be made. The terms 'prevention', 'internal appraisal', 'scrap' and 'warranty' present no difficulties. In the authors' view 'remedial engineering' equates with the simpler and more common 'rework'. 'Product liability' is an external failure cost and the use of the word 'service' in conjunction with 'external appraisal' in the paper suggests it too may be an external failure cost. It is suspected that 'policy' payments which are not included with warranty costs in the paper are not quality costs but there is no way of separating them out.

The comparisons are shown in Tables 8.1 and 8.2 using the format adopted by the journal *Quality* in presenting the findings from their survey.

Table 8.1 Comparison of company 3 quality costs with published data

Cost category	Company 3	Quality *survey data** (formal program)*		Schmidt and Jackson†
		Machinery	*Transport equipment*	
Prevention	7.4	11.0	8.7	2.5
Appraisal	24.0	23.7	45.3	33.7
Internal failure	21.0	39.6	33.2	22.8
External failure	47.6	25.7	12.8	41.0
Total	100	100	100	100
		Sales revenue (%)		
Prevention	0.7	0.49	0.34	0.3
Appraisal	2.3	1.05	1.76	4.0
Internal failure	2.0	1.76	1.29	2.7
External failure	4.1	1.14	0.50	4.8
Total	9.6	4.44	3.89	11.8

*Quality costs survey. *Quality*, June 1977, pp. 20–2 [2].
†Schmidt and Jackson [1].

Examination of the data suggests (even keeping in mind the earlier discussion about the limitations of the data) that the company's situation is closer to that in the Detroit Allison Division of General Motors than to the norms for the industry sectors in which they are grouped. Data compared under informal systems of quality cost collection (i.e. collecting only scrap, rework and warranty costs) suggest that the company not only spends a smaller proportion of its sales revenue on quality than does General Motors, but also that a greater proportion of

Table 8.2 Comparison of company 3 quality costs with published data

Cost category	Quality costs (%)			
	Company 3	Quality survey data* (informal program)		Schmidt and Jackson†
		Machinery	Transport equipment	
Scrap	10	40	39	27
Rework	9	25	40	13
Warranty	81	35	21	59
Total	100	100	100	100
	Sales revenue (%)			
Scrap	0.6	2.5	2.4	1.8
Rework	0.5	1.5	2.5	0.9
Warranty	4.6	2.2	1.3	3.9
Total	5.7	6.2	6.2	6.6

*Quality cost survey. *Quality*, June 1977, pp. 20–2 [2]
†Schmidt and Jackson [1]

its expenditure goes on warranty payments and a smaller proportion on scrap and rework. These relationships are not illogical and are endorsed by the data in the comparison under formal programmes of cost collecton (i.e. prevention, appraisal, internal and external failure costs). Further, these latter data could be interpreted as suggesting that the situation is brought about by the relative expenditures on appraisal. In short, General Motors may spend more on appraisal, giving them more scrap and rework, but allowing fewer non-conforming products to reach the customer. This of course is tantamount to inspecting-in quality, something which cannot be done. Piling heresy upon heresy, these data also suggest that company 3's proportionately greater expenditure on prevention activities in not paying off so far as the customer is concerned though it may be doing so for the company's gross quality costs.

Perhaps these apparent contradictions of the accepted wisdom only serve to reiterate and emphasize the imprudence of making comparisons between sets of data which are not fully understood. In seeking explanations of these apparent anomalies one is taken full circle back to the definitions of quality and quality-related costs as discussed in Chapter 2.

Manufacturers who incur low external failure costs will enjoy a good reputation for customer-perceived quality, even though their in-house performance, with respect to making to specification first time, may be relatively poor, and costly. Among these may be manufacturers with ready outlets for seconds. It may also be true of manufacturers whose products happen to be in vogue among those to whom price (or even value) is not a prime consideration. It should not be imagined that only manufacturers of clothing for High Street outlets, children's toys, popular records, hula-hoops, skate boards, etc. come into this category. Many other items including watches, calculators, jewellery and motor vehicles are examples also. Hence, quite apart from the fact that the figures themselves may not be comparable, the market situations of different companies may make comparisons invalid.

8.7 Presentation and uses of quality cost information

At the highest level of reporting, warranty charges are the only quality-related costs to feature in the profit and loss account of company 3. Because of the method of reporting to reflect movement in warranty provision there is a smoothing effect which obscures the actual month-to-month variation so it is unlikely to provoke any strong reactions. On the face of it, this may appear to be undesirable, but the situations leading to the warranty costs are so far behind the time of the report that they are unlikely to provoke useful action other than to extend the useful work already being done in auditing claims.

In the monthly operating review a quality cost summary, in the form shown in Figure 8.3, is presented without comment. The quality performance summary is expressed in percentage rejects, defects per engine, performance against targets, and cataloguing of defects. Costs do not feature in the performance summary but are raised in the discussion on general quality topics in the report. Here cost is used as the measure of performance for non-conforming parts coming to light during assembly and test operations and also as the ranking criterion for suppliers of rough material. Total labour costs incurred due to non-conforming rough material are expressed as cash and as costs per effective standard hour. Machine shop scrap costs arising from operator errors, machine faults and jig faults are also expressed in this way. Scrap costs are used to rank cost centres and the components causing most problems. Period and year-to-date rankings are shown and scrap costs per effective standard hour accountable to operator error are graphed for the year.

Despite the wealth of cost information and the way it is used the report does not pack a financial punch. The absence of comment on the total cost summary and a welter of technical details from which the cost figures do not stand out clearly from model numbers, numbers inspected, numbers rejected, cost centre numbers, etc. diminish the financial impact of the report considerably. Its messages are more about problems than costs. The quality assurance manager's monthly report to the plant operations director and the parent company's quality director contains the same kinds of costs but does not emphasise them.

		Cost centre	Location						Period								Company 3
		Area Manager	bay						date								quality dept.
		Target	Full year	Jan	Feb	Mar	Apr	May	Jne	Jly	Aug	Sep	Oct	Nov	Dec	
Scrap	Cost £															Report no. and reference no.
	Cost/ESH £															Machine shop scrap Brochure analysis of quality defect report by cost centre QDR O/TO3
	Quantity															
Concessions	Total															Concession Record Quality office
	No. quantity															
	No. – period															
Samples (1st time perf)	Inspected															Sample record book.
	Passed															Foreman log book.
	Failed %															
Final	Inspected															Final inspection
Audit insp. 1st time performance	Passed															Record book
	Failed %															Foreman log book.
Black museum rejects	Individual pt nos															Black museum report
	Total quantity															
Quality cost £	Re-work															Labour accounting report
	Inspection															
Orders Guaranteed	No. of ord. qty															Weekly scrap Patrol report
	Period															
Components audited	Jig test P/F															Audit report
	Audited P/F															
	Sample P/F															
Quality booking errors	No. of batches															Final inspection
	Quantity short															Record book

Figure 8.5 Example of component quality report sheet.

The underlying data leading to the rankings described above are published, as has been described earlier, in a useful quality assurance department report of scrap costs arising from bought-out rough material. In this report cost data are used to rank suppliers, problems and suppliers' problems. It is surprising that this work or its effects does not somehow feature in the purchasing department's performance report.

Finally, it is the monthly quality performance report for the machining shop which promises to use cost data to make the greatest impact. A separate sheet for each work centre features various quality criteria (Figure 8.5). Clearly displayed on the top line is the cost of scrap, which is also expressed as the cost per effective standard hour. Costs of rework and associated inspection costs are included in the report which also indicates target values. The report is updated monthly and there should be no escaping its message.

References

1. Schmidt, J. W. and Jackson, J. F. (1982) Measuring the cost of product quality. *Automot. Eng.*, **90**, (6), 42–8.
2. Anon (1977) Quality cost survey. *Quality*, 20–2.

9
Case study, company 4

9.1 Introduction

Company 4 is one of a subsidiary group of companies owned by a large multi-national company. It manufactures a variety of high-technology products but this case study was confined to a department making metallized polyester film capacitors for use in electronic circuits for blocking and coupling, bypass, and energy reservoir applications. Output is well in excess of 200 million units per year. Sales turnover is difficult to define because a large proportion of the department's output is used by sister companies and by the parent company and is transferred at the factory selling price. However, the total departmental 'turnover' is to be taken around £3 million per year.

The department operates on a two-shift system and employs approximately 120 people. It is essentially a production unit with some technical support under the control of the production manager but with most of its services coming from other departments.

The quality philosophy of the company is determined by the parent multi-national company with whom there is close liaison on technical, financial and quality matters. The philosophy followed is that of Juran [1] and there is widespread use of his videotape teaching package [2]. Despite this there are striking variations in the quality improvements achieved in different parts of the group of companies and it is noticeable that, in general, the greatest improvements have been made where there is direct competition from Japanese manufacturers.

Quality costs had been collected in the department prior to the commencement of the research study. The objective of this study was to find out how the company had set about collecting quality costs of the department and how it used them. The company was looking for a monthly reporting system by which quality performance is measured in terms of real money, and in a way which is more useful than the underlying data and flexible enough to be applied company wide.

Juran's [1] philosophy on quality is that all improvement takes place project by project, so that, again, it is not surprising to hear in the company a great deal about 'the vital few and trivial many' problems and about quality improvement projects. However, improvement projects seem to have been identified, not from quality costs, but from production and quality control problems, and tend to be concentrated on process deficiencies. Hence quality improvement project teams often seem to be supplementing the technical services in firefighting production and technical problems rather than promoting quality.

The Juran principle of using a project by project approach to quality improvement is so deeply ingrained into thinking in company 4 that some of its personnel see little merit in carrying out full quality costings, other than to get a 'snapshot' of total quality costs from time to time just as a reminder of their magnitude. The weakness of this is that such a use does not encourage refinement of costs and all that is produced is a copy of the original snapshot enlarged by inflation. There is also a tendency to fall into the trap of according an 'accurate' status to costs which have been derived from an intensive study carried out over a short period at some earlier date and to fail to revise estimates of technical and engineering inputs. Any snapshots carried out should also be compared with earlier ones to pinpoint areas of improvement.

Quality costs do not feature in the normal management accounting reports of the company. Apart from the various attempts at snapshot costing, the only other reports are those of the multi-discipline project teams, and these leave much to be desired.

The approach used was to become familiar with the technology and the process (which were very different from any of the earlier studies) and then to perform a critique of the existing quality cost collecting and reporting systems in the light of what had been learned from this and other studies. No attempt was made to match the quality cost elements identified by the company with those of BS 6143 [3], though the omission of important types of cost is noted.

9.2 Sources of quality costs

Two sources of fundamental information on quality costs were uncovered at company 4. From the parent company there is a general definition and guidance on what should be included. This is shown alongside the departmental view of the constitution and categorization of quality costs in Figure 9.1.

Quality-related costs are not specifically mentioned in the company's quality manual but it is interesting to note that the manual is by no means concerned only with the activities of personnel involved in quality assurance; it also acknowledges the contributions of administrative, production operators and supervisors, engineering, and technical service staffs in its procedures covering topics such as:

- specifications;
- documentation;
- work instructions;
- machine instructions (including setting and fault analysis);
- production supervisors' responsibilities (including training);
- inspection;
- disposition of non-conforming products.

Technical data for the department show materials loss allowances of 2% on all products and 2–5% processing losses, depending on the product type, for the basic cell preparation stage with further materials allowances and processing loss allowances of 1–5% for different materials and different processing/testing operations. Of course these losses will not necessarily all give rise to quality-related costs but some will, and the costs will be found to be included in the manufacturing cost and the factory selling price.

Discussions with accounts department personnel yielded stage-by-stage manufacturing cost analyses which confirmed the inclusion of 'loss' and 'scrap' allowances detailed in the technical data for the process. 'Loss' is defined as forerunnings, ends and dropouts, whereas process 'scrap' is defined as non-conforming product. Apart from these inclusions in the standard cost, and the quality assurance department budget, the only other obviously quality-related cost identified in the company's financial reporting is income from sales of 'scrap' metals. However, the company's technical engineering personnel work closely with the accounts department to produce cost analyses of products, operations and activities. One such analysis is the inspection/test content of the factory standard price of major product lines.

A survey of the manufacturing processes and the production operations also confirmed 'loss' and 'scrap' levels and the consequential need to plan for more output than is required. The by-now familiar problem of whether test operations costs are necessarily quality costs arose again at a particular processing stage at which the capacitance of cells is tested and they are sorted into tolerance ranges by machine. The reject rate from this test is of the order of 0.05%. The dilemma arises again at the final 'auto-test' stage at which the completed capacitor is electrically tested for capacitance, insulation resistance, high-voltage breakdown, and integrity of contact of leads. The only corrective work

Company categorization	Departmental categorization

Definition: Quality costs are all costs and losses caused by defective products and the cost of special measures and effort to limit these costs and losses.

Quality costs are divided into:
– inspection costs
– prevention costs
– internal failure costs
– external failure costs

Inspection costs are related to:
– material inspection
– incoming inspection
– product inspection by operators
– product inspection by managers
– product inspection by quality department personnel
– environmental tests
– costs of measuring and test equipment

Appraisal:
– material inspection

– product inspection by operators
– product inspection by supervisors
– product inspection by quality people

– environmental tests
– test-machines and operator hours
– regular inspection on normal work

Prevention costs are the expenditures which have been incurred to reduce the chances of failures in the production process via:
– production and maintenance of manufacturing instructions
– production and execution of the quality education plan
– production of quality procedures
– quality audits of internal processes
– quality audits of external suppliers
– execution of quality analysis

Prevention:
– maintenance of manufacturing instructions

– production of quality procedures
– assessment of departmental quality

– quality analysis
– maintenance of test equipment
– calibration

Internal failure costs are costs related to:
– process disturbance due to bad material
– rework of rejected products
– damage during internal transport

Internal failure:

– repairs and rework
– scrap and losses
– extra inspection due to failure
– machine downtime
– engineering repairs

External failure costs are costs related to:
– handling of complaints
– replacement of rejected products
– service claims
– man hours
– materials

External failure
– customer complaint handling

– extra inspection
– rework
– scrap

Figure 9.1 Parent company and departmental quality cost categorization.

observed was overpainting of faulty printing prior to reprinting, and attention to rolls of taped-on capacitors when the number of gaps on the roll exceeded the specification. The taping process was, however, still under development.

An interesting fact which came to light during the study, and which shows the sensitivity of product quality to technological changes, is the effect of introducing a different type of coating on the product. It is also interesting to note that many of the quality problems encountered by the company derive from the metal spraying and resin coating operations (i.e. non-mechanical, non-electrical operations involving flame and powder technologies).

In-process inspection is carried out by personnel who report to the production foreman and the technical input on in-process quality-related matters comes mainly from the department's engineering resources. The role of the quality assurance department is a policing role at final inspection, and dealing with customer complaints. Thus, curiously, the quality assurance department does not include process yield and scrap levels among its measures of quality performance. Its internal measures of quality are numbers of rejected batches (currently 0.8% versus 4% four years ago) and defects per million which is an absolute measure of all defective capacitors reaching the final operation. External measures are provided by sister companies which inspect products before using them, and by two other customer companies which cooperate to the extent of detecting faulty components in circuits, and removing, packing and returning them with full information. Rejection rates for visual and electrical faults are about 30 per million for small capacitors and one per million for larger capacitors. When quality levels are of this order the feedback of data from customers is the only feasible means of quantification. Problems with packaging, labelling, etc. also become the subject of a customer complaint handling procedure.

Other activities which give rise to quality-related costs are quality improvement projects carried out part time by teams of three people, and the coordination of these projects. Special studies on quality-related matters are also undertaken by the company's technical service department. Thus whilst materials usages and appraisal activities appear to be well defined and analysed there are a number of unmeasured technical inputs from a variety of sources, which could make gathering quality costs difficult. However, an excellently thorough study of quality-related costs had been carried out by an engineer in the company two years prior to the work described in this chapter taking place.

9.3 Measurement of quality costs

The company has been measuring quality costs with progressively greater degrees of sophistication since 1970.

In the department which is the subject of this study and chapter a quality costing exercise was carried out during Year A. The investigator, from the company's quality engineering department, after a thorough study of the process listed 41 quality cost elements under the usual failure–appraisal–prevention categories. Further, he set down, for each element, how to calculate its cost, the data sources and named contacts for each data source. The most striking feature of this report is that the cost elements are particular to the company and the manufacturing operation. No attempt is made to fit elements to elements with generic titles.

A number of lessons can be learnt from this excellent quality costing exercise. Firstly, there is no substitute for a detailed thorough examination. Modifications may be made later, if necessary, with hindsight and as experience of applying the model procedure grows. Secondly, people willingly adopt ready-made procedures if the procedure appears to fit their situation. Hence it is very important that the first-off should be soundly based. Thirdly, procedures should be 'user friendly' (that is, the information needed should be readily obtainable from a relatively small number of sources). The costing was developed by examining the process in detail from beginning to end. Only later were cost elements, still operation based, grouped under the prevention–appraisal–failure categories. This grouping was probably done in deference to the received wisdom on the topic because the requirements of a costing system would not have produced elements which fell naturally into such groupings (though the words are useful as a primary checklist when examining activities to find if they are quality related). Indeed it is likely that only those costs which are easily measured and obviously reducible would have emerged (i.e. some failure and some appraisal costs).

This piece of work was built upon later by a quality assurance department engineer assigned to the production department. He carried out a similar exercise (based on three months' data) but combined some of the cost elements, isolated an important extra element and, most importantly, qualified the status of the cost data. Qualification was expressed in two ways. Firstly, costs were labelled A, TD or E, indicating that they were derived from accurate data (i.e. from an exact amount of losses recorded over a reasonable period, or from booked time), from published technical data for the process, or estimated, respectively. Secondly, the cost report specifically highlights the dilemmas of cost allocation which occur at the heal and sort and autotest process stages, namely:

> The time included for operator inspection is the time spent on visual inspection only. There is no inclusion of time spent operating the machines in their test and sort capacity. However, the full machine hours costs have been used, despite healing being a necessary stage in manufacture, and the auto-test machines doing manufacturing jobs such as cropping, unloading from strips and counting into boxes.

At the same time that the latter report was being prepared another quality cost report was being prepared by the department's technical services engineer. This report, which uses the elements defined for the first report (Year A), purports to apply the following year's (Year B) experience to the current year's (Year C) production levels to produce a forecasted expenditure or budget. A similar report has also been prepared by the same author in which Year C experience is applied to the forecasted production levels for Year D.

At company 4 it was noticed that many of the quality problems emanated from two parts of the process which involved flame technology and powder technology respectively. These are effectively foreign technologies in a manufacturing process which uses electrical and mechanical engineering in its principal technologies. When attempting to define quality cost elements, an implicit requirement is that the technologies must be fully understood. Failure to do so may result in the true causes of quality defects being missed, or to accepting lower standards of performance than should be achieved. This is not the case at company 4, which has a wide range of technological expertise available to it from the parent and sister companies, but it is a philosophical point worth noting.

9.4 Comparison of cost reports

Thus there are four reports available containing costs expressed in such a way that they may be compared one with another. For the purpose of comparison the data are shown in two tables. Table 9.1 shows data from the Year A investigation alongside the production department quality cost forecasts for Year B and Year C. The most striking features of these data are, firstly, that many of the figures in the forecasted data appear to have been obtained by simply inflating the original Year A data by 2–3% per annum, and, secondly, that so many of the rates of expenditure are identical for each of the product sizes. On the first point, in only three of the 39 items listed is there a significant change in the rate of expenditure. The three items, which include product losses at the first roller grade and auto-test stages and repair work, are a direct result of process improvement. On the second point, in view of the fact that there are significantly more problems with the smaller version of the product it is surprising that the rates of expenditure are the same for both products. It might have been expected that, for example, the prevention activities and some of the appraisal activities would reflect differences in process status of the two products. Equally, the reasons for some of the differences shown are not obvious either (e.g. epoxy coat operator inspection costs 20% more per unit for the larger product than for the smaller). Perhaps these apparent anomalies merely reflect the quality of the underlying estimated and technically based data.

Table 9.1 Comparison of original and updated costing

Item	Data status	Original costing		Technical service engineer's costings			
		Year A	Year A	Year B	Year C	Year B	Year C
Annual production =		30 m	190 m	70 m	145 m	120 m	100 m
Product type =		7 mm	9 mm	7 mm	9 mm	7 mm	9 mm
1. Winding foil scrap	A	13.8	29.4	14.2	30.3	14.5	30.9
2. Winding cell loss	A	56.6	78.1	58.3	80.4	59.5	82.0
3. Detaping cell loss	A	71.6	57.6	73.7	5.9	7.5	6.0
4. 1st roller grade cell loss	A	130.5	152.3	33.6	39.2	34.3	40.0
5. 1st heal cell loss	A	49.9	58.2	51.4	49.9	52.4	61.0
6. 2nd roller grade cell loss	A	27.3	31.9	28.1	32.8	28.7	33.5
7. 2nd heal cell loss	A	22.6	26.4	23.3	27.2	23.7	27.7
8. Auto-test cell loss	A	1250.6	645.2	776	428.8	601.0	437.4
9. Machine downtime	E	71.0	63.4	73.1	65.3	74.6	66.6
10. Mechanical engineering hours	E	29.8	61.6	29.8	63.4	30.4	64.7
11. Engineering orders	E	11.8	11.8	12.2	12.2	12.4	12.4
12. Stores items	E	32.3	32.3	33.3	33.3	34.0	34.0
13. Toolroom orders	E	19.1	19.1	19.7	19.7	20.1	20.1
14. Mechanical engineering hours	E	194.7	151.3	200.5	155.8	204.5	158.9
15. Toolroom orders	E	12.2	12.2	12.6	12.6	12.9	12.9
16. Electronic engineering hours	E	80.2	80.2	82.9	82.6	84.6	84.3
17. Repairs	TD	1132.1	51.9	291.5	53.5	96.2	54.6
18. Winding operator inspection	TD	53.0	50.0	54.6	51.5	55.7	52.5
19. Roller grade	TD	53.7	53.7	55.3	55.3	56.4	56.4
20. Heal and sort operator inspection	TD	148	183.6	152.4	111.2	155.4	113.4
21. Batch inspection	TD	86.5	86.5	89.1	90.9	90.9	90.9
22. Welding operator inspection	TD	46.0	46.1	47.4	47.5	48.3	48.3
23. Epoxy coat operator inspection	TD	36.0	45.0	37.1	46.4	37.8	47.3
24. Print operator inspection	TD	27.0	27.7	27.8	28.6	29.2	29.2
25. Sillner tape operator inspection	E	127	0	130.8	0	66.7	0
26. In-line quality	TD	170.4	170.4	175.5	175.5	179.0	179.0
27. 100% inspect	A	29.4	29.4	30.3	30.3	30.9	30.9
28. Raw material inspection	A	2.3	2.3	2.4	2.4	2.4	2.4
29. Quality laboratory	E	82.5	82.5	85.0	85.0	86.7	86.7

Item	Data status						
30. Works laboratory	A	9.4	9.4	9.7	9.7	9.9	9.9
31. Auto-test man-hours	TD	159.9	195.9	164.7	164.7	167.9	167.9
32. Auto-test machine hours	TD	707.5	707.5	728.7	728.7	743.0	743.0
33. Heal and sort machine hours	TD	274.5	274.5	282.7	282.8	288.3	288.3
34. Electronic engineering hours	E	20.9	20.9	21.5	21.5	21.9	21.9
35. Engineering orders	E	6.2	6.2	6.4	6.4	6.5	6.5
36. Quality engineering hours	E	23.4	23.4	24.1	24.1	24.6	24.6
37. Quality laboratory	E	54.6	54.6	58.1	58.1	59.3	59.3
38. Technical assistance	A	98.8	98.8	101.8	101.8	103.8	103.8
39. Works laboratory	A	2.6	2.6	2.7	2.7	2.8	2.8

Table 9.2 shows the combined (all-products) cost data from Table 9.1 alongside data from the Year B costing. It is immediately apparent that this latter report shows some substantial differences from the report for the same year compiled by the production department's technical service engineer.

Table 9.2 Comparison of costings of all-products data

Item		Data status	Original costing	Technical service engineers' costing		Quality engineer's costing
			Year A	Year B	Year C	Year B
Annual production =			220 m (m)	215 m	220 m	200 m
1.	Winding foil scrap	A	27.3	25	22	25
2.	Winding cell loss	A	75.1	73.2	69.7	73
3.	Detaping cell loss	A	5.95	6.4	6.8	6
4.	1st roller grade cell loss	A	149.3	37.4	36.9	69
5.	1st heal cell loss	A	57.1	57.1	56.3	83
6.	2nd roller grade cell loss	A	31.3	31.3	30.9	
7.	2nd heal cell loss	A	25.9	25.9	25.5	
8.	Auto-test cell loss	A	727.8	541.8	572	542
9.	Machine downtime	E	64.9	67.8	71	68
10.	Mechanical engineering hours	E	57.3	52.4	46	
11.	Engineering orders	E	11.8	12.2	12.4	
12.	Stores items	E	32.3	33.3	34.0	
13.	Toolroom orders	E	19.1	19.7	20.1	
14.	Mechanical engineering hours	E	157.2	170.4	183.4	212
15.	Toolroom orders	E	12.2	12.6	12.9	78
16.	Electronic engineering hours	E	80.2	82.6	84.5	82
17.	Repairs	TD	199.2	131	77.3	145
18.	Winding operator inspection	TD	28.9	52.5	54.2	68
19.	Roller grade	TD	53.7	55.3	56.4	112
20.	Heal and sort operator inspection	TD	113.6	124.6	135.3	12
21.	Batch inspection	TD	86.5	89.1	901	100
22.	Welding operator inspection	TD	46.1	47.5	48.3	41
23.	Epoxy coat operator inspection	TD	43.7	43.3	42.1	38
24.	Print operator inspection	TD	27.6	28.3	29.2	24
25.	Sillner tape operator inspect	E	(17.2)	(42.5)	(36.3)	40
26.	In-line quality	TD	170.4	175.5	179	162

27.	100% inspect	A	29.4	30.3	30.9	
28.	Raw materal inspection	A	2.3	2.4	2.4	3
29.	Quality laboratory	E	82.5	85	86.7	90
30.	Works laboratory	A	9.4	9.7	9.9	31
31.	Auto-test man-hour	TD	159.9	164.7	167.9	135
32.	Auto-test machine hours	TD	707.5	728.7	743	664
33.	Heal and sort machine hours	TD	274.5	282.7	288.3	271
34.	Electronic engineering hours	E	20.9	21.5	21.9	22
35.	Engineering orders	E	6.2	6.4	6.5	
36.	Quality engineer's hours	E	23.4	24.1	24.6	76
37.	Quality laboratory	E	56.4	58.1	59.3	28
38.	Technical assistance	A	98.8	101.8	103.8	102
39.	Works laboratory	A	2.6	2.7	2.8	

Under the category of failure there is good agreement between the two on product losses. This is to be expected because most of the data are derived from a single intensive study carried out at the time of the original Year A investigation. Exceptions are the winding cell and auto-test losses which are determined daily by counting and check-weighing. In general the losses are corroborated by the process materials efficiency records. There is also good agreement on the costs of various engineering inputs, which suggests that the estimates of the proportion of this effort which is quality related has remained unchanged since the first investigation. Complaint returns and handling is a new element introduced by the quality engineer who has also combined repairs with other elements thus making exact comparison difficult.

In the appraisal category most of the data are from technical data prepared by the technical efficiency department of the company. Both Year B reports should therefore be the same. The fact that they are not, but that in many cases the differences are small, can be accounted for by use of an overall inflation figure in one set of figures (as mentioned earlier) and use of up-to-date technical data in the other. A difference which can not be explained in this way is the factor of two of the cost of roller grade operator inspection. Attention to these machines is only a part-time activity for an operator but an increase in attention time to the machines may well have come about during investigations into high losses at this process stage. In the case of heal and sort operator inspection, where there is a difference of a factor of ten between the reported figures, there has clearly been a change of definition. The definition used in the original investigation clearly included the whole of the machine operator's time. The latest view is that less than 10% of his time is spent on inspection. A surprising difference is a factor of three on works laboratory costs. These costs are charges-in to the department through the cost centre accounting system and hence should be identical.

Under the prevention category, the estimates of engineering and technical service input used in the original investigation still prevail but the quality engineer's estimates of the quality laboratory's and his own contributions to prevention are halved and trebled respectively.

9.5 Discussion of costs

For the purpose of calculating quality costs as fractions of annual sales turnover the latter is taken to be £3 million. Value of scrapped products is the standard price of the product at its process stage. Thus products scrapped before the welding stage are valued at about one-third of the value ascribed to products scrapped during and after the welding operation. Costs of all hourly paid staff include a proportion of the departmental overhead. Thus, for example, inspectors and fitters are costed at approximately twice as much as departmental engineers and supervisors.

Enquiries into costs always yield contradictory information. Company 4 is no exception. Enquiry into the cost of patrol inspection brought answers of 'two men full time' and 'one man 90% of the time' from two people very close to the manufacturing operation who would be expected to know the exact answer. Similarly three people's assessment of the proportion of machine downtime which is quality related are 'most', '85–90%' and '50–50'. Both of these quality topics fall into the 'estimated' category of cost status.

Much of the data used in calculating costs are fixed data (e.g. production level, machine and manning costs) so that the calculation of many costs could be reduced to measuring an operating variable and applying a factor to it. Some such simplification accompanied by judicious combining of elements will almost certainly be necessary if this type of reporting is to become routine in company 4. An analysis of the costing procedure shows the system to require inputs from 16 people working in 11 different departments or sections. It should be possible to reduce the number of contributors to four without sacrificing information or accuracy.

Referring to the quality engineer's Year B data, which are the most reliable after the original investigation, failure costs comprise £159 000 materials and added value losses, £37 800 additional labour costs directly associated with the losses, and a further £88 000 related costs. Many appraisal costs are unavoidable (e.g. operator inspection) and these amount to £214 000 leaving £177 000 as perhaps avoidable. Charges-in to the department under appraisal and prevention headings are challengeable and, possibly, reducible. In the period between this and the original costing there have clearly been improvements in quality performance and the effects on total quality costs are to reduce them by about 5% of sales turnover. Most of the reduction comes from significant reductions in roller grade cell losses, auto-test cell losses and repairs. How real an apparent reduction in appraisal costs and an increase in prevention expenditure may be is difficult to gauge in view of the disparities discussed earlier.

One of the maxims of cost collecting seems to be that, in general, costs need to be large to hold attention. This creates something of a dilemma for the cost collector because large costs are often insensitive to changes. But the collector cannot omit large costs and concentrate only on smaller costs which may readily be seen to change. Hence cost groupings need to be chosen carefully so that cost reductions achieved are displayed in such a way that both the relative achievement and the absolute position are clearly shown. Another dilemma arises from the fact that one-off estimates do not change and that there is no point in collecting costs which do not change. The only way out of this is to measure directly, or through surrogates, those costs which are thought worth collecting.

9.6 Quality cost reporting

Apart from scrap sales in departmental accounts, quality-related costs are reported in only two contexts at company 4. One is the annual quality costs and the other is in quality improvement projects.

The original annual report which was prepared as a special project by an engineer from the company's quality engineering department was endorsed by the production manager and circulated widely in the department, to the quality fraternity on the site, and to the plant director. It comprises a 150 word covering note but otherwise leaves the figures to speak for themselves. The presentation of figures, though neat and clear, is essentially on working papers (i.e. typed format with handwritten figures and hand-drawn Pareto charts) and hence may not create the impact among senior management that such an excellent piece of work deserves. Another weakness is that all costs are expressed as costs per million of the product type so that to arrive at real costs the reader is constantly having to multiply by 140 and by 30 and sum the products. (Ironically the reports obtained by simply inflating the data in this original report are well presented but appear not to have made any impact.) However, the derived list of potential improvement projects does not suffer from either of these defects and clearly achieved its purpose when the top three projects were adopted and brought to successful conclusions.

The second annual report (for Year B), prepared by the quality engineer assigned to the department and incorporating the improvements noted earlier, also has a minimum of words and asks the figures to speak for themselves. Unfortunately, in this case, there has been no detailed analysis of the data leading to possible improvement projects. Nor is there a comparison with the original report to measure changes even though there were substantial improvements via the improvement projects in Year B. Combining the costs of the two main product types serves to obscure high-cost areas to some extent, because they have quite different quality cost rates per million. Clearly the report does not say as much as it could and may not make the impact that the work of compiling it deserves.

The reporting of quality costs in quality improvement project reports is sketchy and incomplete. It is also confusing. The confusion arises partly from poor form design of the quality improvement planning sheets (QUIPS) and partly because of some odd reporting practices. The poor form design contributes to the confusion because the three improvement projects have to share a sheet of A4 paper with customer problem reports such that the financial reporting of all three projects is squeezed into an area of 12 cm × 4 cm. Reporting practices are odd in several respects. At the initiation of the project the annual expenditure and the expected annual savings (and hence the anticipated future annual expenditure) are clearly defined. Two months later, before the first review meeting, the assessment of the annual loss from 'mechanical losses due to poor levelling' had rocketed from £27 510 to £63 360 although it was then currently cruising along at a rate of £27 547 per annum. In the same period the annual expenditure rate of 'Sillner repairs' fell from £43 821 to £29 214 per annum – a considerable improvement until it is learned that the latter figure is based on an output level of two-thirds the original. The expenditure rate was later reduced to £14 600 per annum – but for one-third of the originally specified output level. The changes from expenditure to expenditure rates and the reasons for moving the goal posts are not indicated on the reporting format and must be gleaned from the minutes of quality improvement meetings which monitor the projects and consider these reports. These meetings were held at the intervals at which the QUIPS were produced (indeed the QUIPS predated the meetings by one day). They are attended by leaders of the project teams together with senior managers from the quality, production and site management functions. They are essentially reporting-upwards meetings in which situation and progress are reported, apparently without feedback (as judged by the minutes). It is probably fair to say that the minutes, apart from attendance, could be written before the meeting.

A point arising from the poor quality of reporting at company 4 is that the very fact of there being a multiplicity of reports with conflicting figures, all effectively from within the same department, undermines confidence in all of them, even the best.

A topic which is reported on at the meeting, and one which clearly is regarded by the company as being of the highest importance, is that of customer problems. Although the level of defects is very low (as indicated earlier, the individual capacitors are very cheap) the numbers returned (e.g. 40 000 in three months) plus the cost of personnel dealing with complaints may warrant costing. It is a surprising omission.

Another curious and disappointing feature of company 4 is that it has all the ingredients necessary for preparing excellent quality cost reports for improvement projects and total costs, but it does not do so. It employs high-calibre staff. The matrix organization ensures engineering, technical and quality assurance staff become fully integrated into the manufacturing function whilst maintaining strong links with their respective support functions. Technical engineering staff who provide a wealth of technical and cost data are similarly placed within the accounting function. Overall, the company is extremely well suited to tackle quality cost collection. All the ingredients for successful quality cost reporting are there and all that is needed is some changes to attitudes and the will to do it.

The reasons why the state of quality cost reporting is not far better were not studied specifically. However, a number of matters noted during the study may have some bearing on the situation. Firstly, responsibility for quality seems to be divided. For example, the quality assurance department appeared to be preoccupied with customer-perceived quality, leaving the responsibility for in-house quality to the manufacturing department. The prime responsibility for product and service quality must of course lie with manufacturing departments, but quality assurance departments have a tacit responsibility in all matters relating to quality – especially failure. Secondly, the maverick behaviour of the manufacturing department's technical service engineer, in producing and pushing his own independent sets of data, is but an example of interdepartmental insularity at company 4. Management's acceptance or open reluctance to accept, or acknowledge, other figures, without attempting to determine the truth, is surely another. Thirdly, there was some evidence of a big-company syndrome of no one 'owning' problems, though there was much evidence of willingness to become involved with problems and contribute to solutions. Finally, there is a lack of expressed dissatisfaction on the part of senior management. (This may be related to the previous point about people not owning problems.) An example, quoted in the case study, is the apparent lack of response from members of the senior management team to quality improvement project reports. Quite apart from the poor standard of reporting, there surely must have been aspects of the work (technical, cost, rate of progress, changing priorities, changing targets, etc.) with which they were not entirely satisfied.

9.7 Uses of quality costs

As mentioned earlier, company 4 is an adherent of the Juran [1] philosophy on TQM and quality costs. Very briefly, Juran advocates the use of costs to quantify threats or opportunities, to draw attention, and to initiate cost improvement projects using return on investment as the principal criterion for assessing projects. Hence it is not surprising that the investigator who carried out the original costing exercise did not end with the report described earlier in this chapter. Process, control and cost data were used to prepare cost-based Pareto charts of causes of scrap arising from each of the three principal process stages (i.e. widening, welding and coating) for each of the two major product sizes. Cost-based Pareto charts were also developed for scrap arising from the remaining process stages and untraceable faults. Examples are shown in Figure 9.2

From this information a list of eight improvement projects was developed (Figure 9.3). The basic problems and their associated failure costs are listed against the savings to be made. At this stage the whole of the particular failure cost was seen as a potential saving. The potential savings from eliminating the auto-test scrap elements listed are about 35% of the total auto-test scrap value and the total potential savings listed represent 30% and 13.7% of the failure costs and total quality costs respectively.

The top three problems were made the subject of quality cost improvement projects with teams, leaders, timescales, control criteria, and expected savings specified. Progress was formally reported after four, seven, ten and 12 months via a simple project reporting format and at quality improvement meetings with members of the senior management team.

Meanwhile, the manufacturing department's technical services engineer, anticipating the quality engineer's cost report for 1983, produced a quality improvement plan in which was listed an assortment of specific solutions to problems, proposals for trials of new techniques and materials, and a call for further improvement to levelling of products prior to coating. The list was later condensed from 16 to five items with unexplained costs and appended to the cost report referred to earlier (which was obtained by inflating costs in the original report). The condensed plan or 'proposed strategy' must not have been adopted because the items appear again (albeit with different costs) appended to the next annual report by inflation.

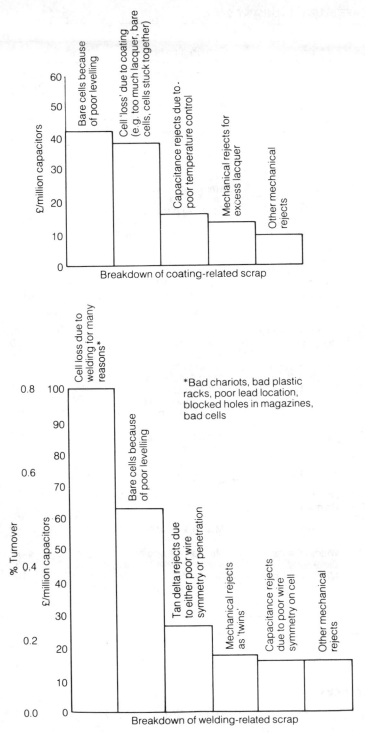

Figure 9.2 Pareto chart examples.

Number	Problem	Contribution from	£/annum	
1	Sillner Repairs	Machine Operator End Control	20364 12042	
				32405
2	Winding faults	9 mm 1st rollergrade cell loss 7 mm 1st rollergrade cell loss	28880 3900	
				32780
3	Levelling	9 mm Autotest scrap (due to weld) 9 mm Autotest scrap (due to epoxy coat) 7 mm Autotest scrap (due to weld) 7 mm Autotest scrap (due to epoxy coat) 9 mm Autotest level scrap	11970 7980 1470 960 5130	
				27510
4	Unexplained Capacitance Rejects	9 mm Autotest scrap 7 mm Autotest scrap	14630 2970	
				17600
5	Wire Symmetry or Penetration	9 mm Autotest scrap (tan delta) 9 mm Autotest scrap (capacitance) 7 mm Autotest scrap (tan delta) 7 mm Autotest scrap (capacitance)	5130 3040 5310 630	
				14110
6	Detaping	9 mm Stage loss 7 mm Stage loss	11020 2160	
				13180
7	Winding faults: Dropping foil, No mylar pickup Doubles	Mechanical engineering hours 9 mm Machine downtime hours 9 mm Mechanical engineering hours 7 mm Machine downtime hours 7 mm	5135 1182 268 40	
				6625
8	Welding faults: Weak weld Missing weld	Mechanical engineering hours Machine downtime 9 mm Machine downtime 7 mm	4472 1187 196	
				5855

Figure 9.3 List of potential improvement projects.

References

1. Juran, J. M. (ed.) (1988) *Quality Control Handbook*, McGraw-Hill, New York.

2. Juran, J. M. (1979) *Quality Management Work Book*, Juran Enterprises, New York.
3. BS 6143 (1981) *The Determination and Use of Quality-Related Costs*, British Standards Institution, London.

10
Setting up a quality costing system

10.1 Introduction

This short concluding chapter of quality costing, by drawing on the previous nine chapters, offers a number of pointers to organizations on how they might approach the collection, analysis and reporting of quality costs.

10.2 Quality costing pointers

It is unlikely that an organization's management accounts will contain the necessary information in the right form. Hence it is essential to involve accountants from the outset. It is recommended that the quality cost collector attempts to make friends with the accountants and is careful not to antagonize them.

There is no point in collecting quality-related costs just to see what they may reveal. The purpose of quality costing should be clarified at the start of the project as this may influence the strategy of the exercise and will help to avoid difficulties later. If, for example, the main objective of the exercise is to identify high-cost problem areas, approximate costs will suffice. If, on the other hand, the purpose is to set a percentage cost-reduction target on the organization's total quality-related costs, it will be necessary to identify and measure all the contributing cost elements in order to be sure that costs are reduced and not simply transferred elsewhere.

It will also be necessary to decide how to deal with overheads, since many quality-related costs are normally included as part of the overhead, whilst others are treated as direct costs and attract a proportion of overheads. Failure to clarify this can lead to a gross distortion of the picture derived from the quality-related cost analysis. It is also easy to fall into the trap of double-counting. For these and other reasons quality-related costs should be made the subject of a memorandum account. However, the costs should not include recovery of overheads in calculating costs of personnel.

Another area of difficulty is deciding whether some activities, usually of a setting-up, testing or running-in type, are quality activities or an integral and essential part of the production/operations activity. These costs often can be substantial and can alter quite markedly the relative proportions of quality-related costs categories. There are also factors which serve to ensure the basic utility of the product and/or service, guard against errors, and protect and preserve product and service quality. Examples are the use of design codes, preparation of engineering, technical and administrative systems and procedures, capital premiums on machinery, and equipment, document and drawing controls, and handling and storage practices. Whether such factors give rise to costs which may be regarded as being quality related is a matter for judgement in individual cases. These problems need to be discussed with purchasing, engineering, production/operations, and accountancy personnel, as appropriate, in order to resolve them. There is little doubt that deciding which activities should be included under the quality-related cost umbrella is by no means straightforward and there are many grey areas. Some quality assurance managers have a tendency to include costs that are difficult to justify as being quality related and over which they have no control or influence. This overzealousness should be guarded against.

One of the maxims of quality cost collection seems to be that, in general, costs need to be large to hold the attention of people. Size is often regarded as being synonymous with importance, though it is size coupled with relevance and potential for reduction which determines the real importance of costs. Clearly it may be much more advantageous to pursue a small percentage in a large cost than a large reduction in a small cost, depending on the ease of achievement. This creates something of a dilemma for the cost collector because large costs are often insensitive to changes. But the collector cannot omit large costs and concentrate only on smaller costs which may be readily seen to change. Hence cost groupings need to be chosen carefully so that the cost reductions which are achieved are displayed in such a way that both the relative achievement and absolute position are clearly shown. Another dilemma facing the cost collector arises from the fact that one-off estimates of quality costs tend not to change and some people take the view that there is no point in collecting costs which do not change.

The only way out of this dilemma is to measure directly, or through surrogates, those costs which it is thought worth collecting.

A checklist of quality cost elements can provide a useful starting point for the cost collection exercise. However, there is no substitute for a thorough analysis of all an organization's activities and some key elements may be missed if only this method is used. BS 6143 provides such a list of elements under the cost categories of prevention, appraisal, internal failure and external failure. In some organizations cost elements have been identified by scanning the quality costing literature, and other organizations from analysis of their processes using, for example, a process cost model as typically outlined in BS 6143, have identified the costs incurred from not getting operations right the first time.

In the absence of an established quality-related cost reporting system, start by looking into failure costs, namely:

- failure costs attributable to suppliers or subcontractors:
- in-house mistakes, scrap, rework, and rectification costs;
- downgraded products or 'seconds';
- free repairs or replacements for products or services which are defective as delivered;
- warranty and guarantee costs;
- litigation costs.

Follow this by enquiring into the costs of inspection, checks, false starts, disruption to routine production and operations activities, and quality-related inefficiencies built into standard costs. Record how quality-related costs are computed so that the validity of comparisons made across departments, products, processes or time may be checked.

When cost information is available analyse it. Attribute costs to department, defect type, product, cause, supplier, etc. Identify responsibility for costs with functions and people. Rank problems and cost reduction projects by size and importance. Integrate the collection, analysis and reporting of quality-related costs into the company accounting system – but aim to keep paperwork to a minimum.

The reporting of quality costs should be such that the costs make an impact and the data used to their full potential. Consideration needs to be given to issues such as: a standardized reporting format; clarity and simplicity of reporting with minimum use of words; the quality costs data are well presented; the data are complete; and the decisions to be taken by management from the reported data are clear. The summarized data should be supported by detailed information – especially the failure costs. Attention should be given to the use of histograms and pie charts with standard range and scales. This ensures that the relative magnitude of cost elements plotted on separate charts is kept in perspective, thus making comparisons and judgements easier. The quality costs should always be separated from other aspects of product and service quality and presented in the context of other costs.

Successful quality costing systems, as an everyday feature of an organization's management activities, take a long time to establish. It can take up to five years to reach the status of credibility and usefulness that should be expected of data featured in a management information system. A measure of the organizational status of quality costing is if it features in the quality manual.

10.3 Quality costing do's and don'ts

A few do's and don'ts which may help organizations to avoid some of the difficulties and traps typically encountered in a quality cost collection exercise are shown below.

DO'S

- Get the purpose and the strategy clear at the start.
- Report only costs produced or endorsed by the accounts departments.
- Make a friend of the accountant.
- Get data and costs from standard data wherever possible.
- Seek independent corroboration of any data which are doubtful.
- Avoid getting bogged down with trying to understand all the underlying details.
- Start with failure costs.
- Consider appraisal costs as a target for cost reduction.
- Consider ease of collection and start with the easiest cost elements.
- Ensure that any first-off quality costing is soundly based.
- Refine large costs rather than attempt to quantify small unknown costs.
- Concentrate on costs that do or can change with quality improvement activities.
- Remember that rigid systems make for easier quality cost collection.
- Analyse and report costs clearly in a business context.
- Relate quality costs to the profit of the organization.
- Avoid a multiplicity of quality costing reports.
- Consider displaying, as part of an organization's visual management system, the main elements of failure.
- Consider reporting warranty and guarantee payments as a separate quality cost category.
- Treat 'economic cost of quality' models with suspicion; their validity is disputed.

DON'TS

- Forget that there are many complexities and difficulties in the measurement and collection of quality-related costs.
- Go it alone – seek accounting, engineering and technical help as appropriate.
- Expect accountants to take the initiative.
- Expect accountants to arbitrate on what is, or is not, quality related; accountants dread dealing with 'grey areas'.
- Believe that standard accounting systems will yield the information needed; there is a certain inaptness of some conventional accounting systems for dealing with quality-related costing.
- Forget that the cost collector has often to adopt a 'Sherlock Holmes' type of approach in sifting through the data in order to identify costs which are quality related.
- Underestimate the difficulties with definitions of quality costs.
- Be too ambitious – start small.
- Expect too much from the first attempt; any such attempt is likely to underestimate the costs.
- Lose sight of the fact that it is primarily a cost collection exercise.
- Agonize over relatively trifling costs; keep the cost elements and/or categories in perspective.
- Use guesses – not even informed guesses.
- Make comparisons unless you can guarantee comparability.
- Assume straightforward operations will necessarily be easy to cost.
- Overlook the fact that transactions between companies and their customers and suppliers are often as difficult to cost as in-house transactions.
- Forget that prevention is the most difficult category to cost.
- Deduct from quality costs income from scrap.
- Forget that costs derived from estimates of time or from special intensive studies often do not get revised.
- Concentrate exclusively on what is already known.
- Overlook the fact that concessions, design, document and engineering changes are a major source of quality-related costs which often do not receive the attention they merit.
- Be constrained by the traditional prevention–appraisal–failure categorization of quality costs; there are other categorizations which are closer to standard business practices.

10.4 Concluding summary

In conclusion, total quality management as a key organizational business parameter and strategy is here to stay, and needs to be seen and treated by organizations as such. One of the factors in promoting a process of continuous quality improvement is the collection, reporting and use of quality-related cost information. Quality costs need to be formally stated as part of an organization's operational planning and budgetary system and operated as such by executives.

The task of quality costing is not easy. There may be internal opposition to the concept and obscuration of the data, but those individuals and organizations who have persevered and succeeded have found the exercise very rewarding – indeed some see it as vital if they are to remain profitable in an increasingly competitive market. The difficulties associated with quality costing touched upon in this book should not be regarded as a deterrent by organizations considering quality cost collection. Those who have undertaken quality costing have benefited from the experience and from the findings. A number of organizations claim that quality costing has assisted them in achieving world-class status. Many organizations are surprised when they learn of the potential savings and soon want to develop their quality-related costing systems to gain greater benefits and cost control. However, they should not overlook the fact that improvements in quality performance do not necessarily produce pro rata changes in quality-related costs.

Organizations should seek help if they need it. Collection and use of quality-related costs can and does pay off. However, it should not be forgotten that it is not enough to have the necessary mechanism for collecting quality-related costs in place; it is also necessary for the organization's senior management team to have the will to carry the quality costing out and to use the data.

Index